Praise for *Parents Rising*

Filled to the brim with biblical and well-grounded guiding principles and ideas for putting those principles into practice, this book will help parents become the loving and wise leaders that God has called them to be and that their kids need them to be.

TODD CARTMELL
Author of *8 Simple Tools for Raising Great Kids*

Arlene Pellicane does it again! She hits on a critical topic and calls us all to rise up to the task of parenting God's way! In our "empowering" world, something is being lost: respect. God's kingdom is a kingdom. It is not a democracy. He expects us to operate in respect and submission to a hierarchy of authority. A child who is not raised to do so may fit in, but he or she will not rise to the task of being godly in a godless culture. Many of the single sentences Arlene has written in here are alone worth the cost of the entire book.

DANNAH GRESH
Bestselling author and creator of *Secret Keeper Girl*

I've thought about writing a book called *Be the Parent*. I don't have to. Arlene has. This is a strong and necessary book. Arlene masterfully manages to be true to her statement: "This book isn't aimed at producing guilt; it's about promoting growth." The ideas from experts she interviewed, her own illustrations, and her refreshing use of Scripture will empower you. Her very practical ideas will equip you to lead. For the sake of your family, read this now.

KATHY KOCH
Founder/President of Celebrate Kids, Inc.
Author of *Screens and Teens: Connecting with Our Kids in a Wireless World*

I loved *Parents Rising* and so will you! Arlene Pellicane empowers you as a parent, explains what it means to be a parent, and shows you how to do the job right . . . and biblically.

DAVID CLARKE
Christian psychologist, speaker, and the author of 11 books, including *Honey, We Need to Talk*

Given the state of the family today, *Parents Rising* is a crucial book for every parent. Full of biblical wisdom, applicable research, and practical ideas for everyday families, this book is a must-read, regardless of how long you have been on the parenting journey. Our role and responsibility is too crucial not to rise up! We love this book!

PATRICK AND RUTH SCHWENK
Founders of TheBetterMom.com, FortheFamily.org, and authors of *For Better or For Kids: A Vow to Love Your Spouse with Kids in the House*

How healthy is your home? This is the question that Arlene Pellicane asks readers at the opening of her newest book, *Parents Rising*. As the mother of seven children myself, I find I am always asking myself this question. Even seasoned parents get weary—and weary parents lose perspective. Arlene hits the nail on the head with her call back to Christ-honoring, common-sense parenting in which the parents assume the role God has given them and prepare to launch mature (or at the very least maturing!) young adults into the world to shine for Christ. She'll remind you of the priorities given in God's Word for parents—starting with remembering what the highest priority should be. If you've got children, this is a must-read. It gets right to the heart of the goal of parenting in "such a time as this."

HEIDI ST. JOHN
Speaker and author of *Becoming Mom Strong*

Parents Rising is a great book for parents to study and discuss in a small group format. Several timely topics are set up for great discussion and brainstorming for parents. There are many practical examples you can use right away and integrate into your day-to-day parenting.

TIMOTHY JOHANSON
Associate Professor of Pediatrics, University of Arizona College of Medicine Coauthor of *GIST: The Essence of Raising Life-Ready Kids*

Over the years, I have been so impressed with Arlene's wisdom and insight as an author, speaker, and friend. In this great new book, she describes how parenting takes not only building expectations through rules, but also deep relationship and connection with your kids. These pages will walk you through the essential steps to building a strong family, at every step and every stage of life.

SHAUNTI FELDHAHN
Bestselling author of *For Women Only* and *For Parents Only*

Parents Rising is a much-needed resource for your family and an opportunity to educate others with the effective strategies it provides. Arlene Pellicane is a woman whose heart can be trusted, her efficiency in tackling today's parenting challenges makes her the voice of a generation. Arlene's wealth of diligent research and her own vulnerable, heartfelt sharing will allow parents to safely consider their own need for growth. My fervent prayer is that her advice and wise counsel will be embraced, practiced, and shared, leading to parents rising to her challenge to raise kids who love God, respect authority, and value what's right!

TRACEY EYSTER
Founder, MomLifeToday.com and Mom Camp
Author of *Be the Mom* and coauthor of LifeWay's Beautiful Mess Bible study

Parenting is about leadership and your kids desperately need you to be their leader. Don't know how to do that? Arlene will equip you to be the leader your kids need you to be.

JILL SAVAGE
Coauthor of *No More Perfect Kids*, author of *Real Moms . . . Real Jesus*

Do you ever feel discouraged, overwhelmed, or defeated as a parent? Sometimes I do. That's why I'm grateful for books like *Parents Rising*. Arlene Pellicane has written an encouraging and practical read that's sure to inspire, challenge, and equip us all to be more confident parents.

ASHLEIGH SLATER
Author of *Team Us* and *Braving Sorrow Together*

Bravo! The first time I heard Arlene give this message in front of thousands on Mother's Day, both my husband and myself stood to our feet in enthusiastic applause. This is a must-hear, must-read, must-apply message for EVERY parent! The next generation—and generations to come—are depending on all of us who are parents (and grandparents) to RISE UP and live out the high calling, the honor and God-given privilege of leading our children in the ways of God. Arlene Pellicane shows us how—and why— we all must become Parents Rising!

PAM AND BILL FARREL
Authors of 45 books including bestselling *Men Are Like Waffles, Women Are Like Spaghetti; 10 Best Decisions a Parent Can Make;* and *10 Questions Your Kids Ask About Sex: Answers to Have Ready*

Arlene Pelicane calls moms and dads to rise up with courage and confidence to parent with the end goal in mind—children who become responsible, godly adults with character, virtue, and wings to soar. She has her pulse on the struggles of raising godly children in an ungodly culture, and clears a path through the underbrush of multimedia influence to place their feet on a solid foundation of biblical principles. I love this book!

SHARON JAYNES
Bestselling author of *The Power of a Woman's Words* and *Enough: Silencing the Lies that Steal Your Confidence*

Do you want to become a confident parent? Do you want your children to become all that God created them to be? Then *Parents Rising* is a must-read for you and, I believe, for every parent. God has a mighty plan for this next generation! So we must rise up and be the parents God has called us to be. Arlene has the amazing gift of sharing her expertise in parenting with great wisdom, a sense of humor and deep truths that make this book an insightful read. I could easily read her book over and over again. All eight strategies are filled with examples any parent can easily begin to apply today. Witness God transform your home and family to be a place where His love, joy, peace, and purpose grow daily. Arlene brings in examples from other experts that will also encourage you and your children to go forward with a mighty purpose and plan. As you read this book, I believe you will move from survival mode to impactful mode. God's desire is to bless you as a parent and for your children to become adults who confidently go forward in their lives following God's incredible plan for them. This is the time for us to rise up and say "as for me and my household, we will serve the LORD" (Josh. 24:15).

SALLY BURKE
President of Moms in Prayer International
Author of *Unshaken* book and study guide

PARENTS RISING

8 STRATEGIES FOR RAISING KIDS WHO LOVE GOD, RESPECT AUTHORITY, AND VALUE WHAT'S RIGHT

ARLENE PELLICANE

MOODY PUBLISHERS

CHICAGO

Edited by Annette LaPlaca
Author photo: Anthony Amorteguy
Interior Design: Ragont Design
Cover Design: Evangela BeSharpCreative LLC
Cover photo of family copyright © 2016 by Lacheev / iStock (588959064). All rights reserved.

Library of Congress Cataloging-in-Publication Data
Names: Pellicane, Arlene, 1971- author.
Title: Parents rising : 8 strategies for raising kids who love God, respect authority, and value what's right / Arlene Pellicane.
Description: Chicago : Moody Publishers, 2018. | Includes bibliographical references.
Identifiers: LCCN 2018006411 (print) | LCCN 2017056584 (ebook) | ISBN 9780802496263 (ebook) | ISBN 9780802416605
Subjects: LCSH: Parenting--Religious aspects--Christianity. | Child rearing--Religious aspects--Christianity. | Christian education of children. | Christianity and culture.
Classification: LCC BV4529 (print) | LCC BV4529 .P426 2018 (ebook) | DDC 248.8/45--dc23
LC record available at https://lccn.loc.gov/2018006411

ISBN: 978-0-8024-1660-5

We hope you enjoy this book from Moody Publishers. Our goal is to provide high-quality, thought-provoking books and products that connect truth to your real needs and challenges. For more information on other books and products written and produced from a biblical perspective, go to www.moodypublishers.com or write to:

Moody Publishers
820 N. LaSalle Boulevard
Chicago, IL 60610

3 5 7 9 10 8 6 4 2

Printed in the United States of America

For Ethan, Noelle, and Lucy

and the generations who will follow

Contents

FOREWORD

Not much is recorded about the childhood of Jesus. However, Luke did say, "Jesus grew in wisdom and stature, and in favor with God and man" (Luke 2:52). Meeting a child's physical needs, while demanding, is not typically overwhelming. As long as parents can keep the food coming and see that the child gets enough sleep and exercise, they will likely raise a healthy child.

Most parents are genuinely concerned about their child's education. They will do extensive research to determine the options open in their community. Then they place the child in the educational setting they think will best help the child gain knowledge and wisdom.

However, many parents give less attention to rearing children who are emotionally, socially, and spiritually healthy. While physical health and education are foundational, without emotional, social, and spiritual health, a child is not likely to reach his potential as an adult. We all know adults who are physically strong and highly educated but fail in life because they cannot relate to people, cannot process their emotions, and have no relationship with God.

So, if you are looking for help in rearing kids who love God, respect authority, and value what's right, you have a friend in Arlene Pellicane. In *Parents Rising*, Arlene calls parents to step up to the plate and give full attention to the emotional, social, and spiritual needs of children.

This is not a book on the philosophy of childrearing. It is a practical book drawn from Arlene's own experience in rearing three children and her extensive interviews with other parents and authors. I suggest that, as parents, you read one of the eight strategies each week and discuss what changes you might make to be more effective in rearing children who will face adulthood with confidence. If you are a single parent, you might read this book with a friend or discuss with a mentor. With the Group Discussion Questions, the book also lends itself to small group settings. This is not simply a book to be read, but one to be applied in real life. You and your children will be much healthier and happier as a result.

GARY CHAPMAN
Author of *The 5 Love Languages*®

INTRODUCTION:

Why You Must Rise

When all that generation had been gathered to their fathers,
another generation arose after them who did not know
the Lord nor the work which He had done for Israel.

Judges 2:10 (NKJV)

They were two words that certainly got my attention: *Make me.*

I was volunteering at my children's elementary school when I heard this girl challenge an adult who instructed her to get in line.

"Please get in line," the adult repeated in an exasperated tone.

"Make me," she repeated, not moving a muscle.

This is a vivid example of how "empowering children" can backfire. That child was too empowered! Can you imagine your grandmother displaying that much audacity and attitude toward an authority in a school setting? I can't picture my grandma ever conducting herself in such a brash manner.

What has happened in recent generations to introduce some bad, bold changes in children? Why are kids more demanding, entitled, prone to attention problems, and emotionally fragile than they were in previous generations? Kids are often exerting their voices loudly while their parents are stifling and questioning theirs.

Parents have lost their way.

I was speaking at a middle school about raising relational kids in a screen-driven world. I gave the parents this action step: collect your children's phones and devices every night. A man walked up to me after the presentation, shook my hand, and thanked me. "I've been afraid to take phones away at night," he said. "But I've known it's the right thing to do, and now I'm going to do it."

I thought about his words long after my talk. That stronglooking dad was unsure and afraid. He needed a voice of encouragement to affirm his parenting instincts were good, that he was on the right track. Good parenting today often runs against the grain of cultural norms, and sometimes we need to know we're not alone in order to persist. Common sense can become overshadowed by compassion. Children mostly need wisdom and guidance from their parents, not pity or indulgence.

I have certainly felt lost and overwhelmed as a parent. I remember when my kids were younger, I would seek solace in the only private place I could find—the bathroom. When my firstborn, Ethan, was two, he thought it was funny to turn off the bathroom's light, close the door, and leave me in the dark. I could hear him giggling on the other side, but it was still fine with me! I just wanted to sit alone for a few minutes, even if that meant being in the dark. I admit it's often much easier to hide from your kids than to rise and engage them.

YOU'VE BEEN PROMOTED

If you look up the word *rise* in the dictionary, you'll find many inspiring definitions that can apply in the context of parenting. You, Mom and Dad, are about "to move from a lower to a higher position," "to attain a higher level or rank" and experience "an upward movement."[1] Cue the sweeping movie theme music. All rise for your promotion!

You are the leader of your home simply by being who you are. You don't have to take a course, pass a test, attain perfection, or be born with a certain pedigree. You are the parent of your child, which makes you, by virtue, automatically one deserving of honor and respect. First you must believe this yourself; then you must make your children believe it too.

I realize that getting your kids to recognize and respect your authority is no small task. As an anonymous quote says, "The toughest thing about raising kids is convincing them you have seniority." Combine the dogged persistence of a child with the lack of conviction in an adult, and you have a recipe for ruin. It's all too easy to slide into a pattern that leaves you taking orders from your kids instead of the other way around. So how can you exude the necessary strength, even when you don't necessarily *feel* strong? Help is on the way.

You are the leader of your home simply by being who you are.

You're going to hear more about our puppy—as our canine member looms large in our family life—but for now let me say I had to learn to be calm and assertive and act like a pack leader with our new furry friend. I needed to carry myself with confidence, even though, as a first-time dog owner, I knew very little by experience. My husband, James, grew up with a poodle, so he acted as our Commander-in-Chief-of-the-Canine.

Many parents are more comfortable being buddies with their kids than pack leaders. That friend-to-friend relationship can feel a lot more comfortable than wielding authority. When parents create waves, they get rocked as well as the kids do—and it's not always pleasant. But children need leaders, not tall friends. Rebellion grows when authority is absent. When parents relinquish control, mutiny inevitably follows.

Just think of what happens when a teacher leaves the classroom for five minutes. Kids talk, get out of their seats, throw paper airplanes, start trashing the room. Can you picture the mess?

The same is true in a home. If you're checked out with your phone, watching TV, or working all the time, your children will start making the rules. When you vacate your role as mom or dad for even a few moments, your children will take advantage. The health of a family rises and falls with leadership.

OUR STATE OF DEPENDENCE

We all want our much-loved children to grow up into a life of godliness and morality. But our children won't drift into a life of godliness and morality by accident. Because of the morally bankrupt world we live in, it takes a great deal of intentional parenting to provide some structure and spiritual handrails to guide our children toward lives submitted to God.

The Barna Group surveyed evangelical Christians—not the unchurched—and discovered that 54 percent do not believe in absolute truth.[2] In other words, that's more than half the professing evangelicals unconvinced of the absolute authority of God's Word! In the next twenty-four hours in America, a thousand unwed teens will become pregnant, five hundred adolescents will begin using drugs, and six youths will commit suicide.[3] In 2013, the government's Centers for Disease Control and Prevention reported the abortion rate was two hundred abortions for one thousand live births.[4] Of the babies born, four out of ten will be born to a single mom.[5]

We can get numb to statistics, but there's a story and brokenness behind every one of these statistics. In order for us to rise as parents in this generation, we must begin on our knees. Our independence from the bondage of sin comes from our absolute dependence on almighty God. Jerusalem lay in ruin when these words were written in Lamentations 2:19: "Arise, cry out in the night, as the watches of the night begin; pour out your heart like water in the presence of the Lord. Lift up your hands to him for the lives of your children."

You won't gain the hearts of your children by blowing commands with a whistle like Captain von Trapp did in *The Sound of Music*. You won't win them over by acting as a harsh tyrant or treating parenting as a spectator sport. You'll gain their hearts by praying for them faithfully and fervently. The kingdom of God works differently from the way the world works. Becoming a leader in your home is about becoming a servant. If Jesus Himself came to serve, humble service is for us too.

Servant leadership may sound like an oxymoron, like "jumbo shrimp." How are you supposed to lead and serve at the same time? My husband, James, likes to call it being a "benevolent dictator." You are softhearted toward your children, putting their needs above your own, while providing strong guidance. You acknowledge you don't possess the answers, but you know the One who does. Psalm 127:1 guides your life: "Unless the LORD builds the house, the builders labor in vain. Unless the LORD watches over the city, the guards stand watch in vain." Our efforts prove fruitless without God's oversight and guidance in all of them.

Scripture promises that the Lord exalts the humble and puts down the proud (1 Peter 5:5). Which kind of parent do you hope to be, humble or proud? When we choose to humble ourselves in prayer and dependence on God, He will lift us up. Going back to some of the many dictionary definitions of *rise*, we will "get up from lying, kneeling, or sitting" and "become heartened or elated."[6] Like

We've just got to look in the right place for help—to God, the Source of wisdom.

the meaning of *rise* carried in the phrase *the sun rises,* help will appear above the horizon! We've just got to look in the right place for help—not down to our phones for life's answers or backward to past mistakes, but up to God, the Source of wisdom.

YOUR EPIC WIN

There was a colorfully painted van in my neighbor's driveway. I'll change the company name to protect the innocent, but it could have been "Poop and Scoop." It was a professional dog waste removal service. Only in America could some entrepreneur build a profitable business out of scooping the waste of residential doggies! Wouldn't it be nice if we could outsource the unpleasant parts of parenting to someone else?

The dog service website described their pricing. A onetime cleanup with low accumulation was $50, and moderate accumulation was $60. For heavy accumulation, it simply said, "Call for quote." You know the yard is in bad shape if you have to call for a quote! Perhaps your parenting could use a "onetime cleanup" to restore order and balance. Maybe you long to jettison a tape of some toxic thoughts running through your mind, like, "I could never get my kids to do that!" or, "I'm such a failure!" There isn't a colorfully painted van with a super nanny on the way to fix your home life—and that's okay. You are the one who has the power to make changes and clean things up around your home. You can do this.

Parents, we must rise!

This book is about letting your old, broken ways of parenting expire. One of the definitions of *rise* is "to return from death."[7] With God's help, we will put fearful, apathetic, selfish, defeatist ways to death, and return with new attitudes and strategies in line with God's Word. You are not stuck in your present family reality. Before you start comparing yourself unfavorably to others, or criticizing yourself for falling short, hear me out. This book isn't aimed at producing guilt; it's about promoting growth.

Listen to Zig Ziglar's wise words: "Failure is an event, not a person."[8] We will fall down as parents, but we must continue to brush ourselves off, learn from our mistakes, and rise again. Rising also means "to exert oneself **You can raise** to meet a challenge."[9] Parenting is one of the **godly kids in a** most challenging endeavors you'll ever begin, **godless culture.** but with God, hope abounds. As long as your children are under your roof, you have time to leverage the power of good parenting. You can raise godly kids in a godless culture.

An epic win for your family lies ahead in the future. Heroes are men and women who perform deeds of valor. They are empowered by God. Their actions are important to the history of a nation and people. Can you imagine what your community would look like if parents acted heroically to intervene for their children spiritually, mentally, emotionally, and physically? What if parents up and down your street started having big, impressive wins in their households? How would that change the vibe of your neighborhood, school, church, city, and beyond?

This epic transformation begins with you.

Will you rise up as a parent and join an army of other parents who are ready to lead? Another definition of *rise* is "an increase in amount, number, or volume."[10] The number of parents who raise kids who love God, respect authority, and value what's right must increase for the sake of your children, and the generations that follow. There's too much at stake in eternity to sit on the sidelines or get sidetracked on a smartphone. As we reject passive parenting, we can rise to vibrantly pass on faith in Christ and biblical values before it's too late.

Looking at a snapshot of my kids taken just one year ago on the last day of school, it struck me how much they had grown. In the photo, Ethan is wearing a NASA shirt that, of course, doesn't fit anymore. He no longer looks like that boy. Good grief, he shaves now! The girls were wearing matching T-shirts and carrying matching pink backpacks. By next year, Ethan will begin high school, Noelle middle school, and Lucy the lone and last Pellicane in elementary school.

Parenting is filled with firsts and lasts. Some bring laughter, and others bring tears. Your child's first steps. The first tooth lost. The first progress report. The last time you watch your child play soccer. The last Father-Daughter Dance. The last day you drive your child to school.

Each day counts. Let's begin this journey of rising up to meet the challenges ahead. It's time to find our way back as parents.

Quiz:
How Healthy Is Your Home?

Take this self-assessment to get a quick overview of your current parenting.

1. My children could have a screen-free, no-Wi-Fi weekend without any problems.

   Yes   No

2. My children show honor to me as a parent.

   Yes   No

3. I enforce house rules and boundaries; my kids know I cannot be swayed.

   Yes   No

4. I pray with my children every day.

   Yes   No

5. We eat at least five screen-free meals per week together as a family.

   Yes   No

6. I enjoy one activity or more with my kids each week (shooting hoops, playing a board game, riding bikes, taking a walk, working on a puzzle, etc.).

    Yes   No

7. I push my children to learn appropriate life skills for their ages such as doing laundry(for younger kids) and managing money (for teens).

    Yes   No

8a. If you are married: I make love to my spouse at least once a week.

    Yes   No

8b. If you are single: I speak positively about marriage and introduce my children to people with strong marriages.

    Yes   No

Total the number of yes answers:

1–4: It's time to make needed repairs. Your foundation is weak, but don't worry, it can be reinforced. You will be gaining skills to become a more effective leader in your home.

5–6: You have a few home-improvement projects that need attention. As you make key changes, you will see a big difference in how your children respond to you.

7–8: You are building on a solid foundation. With a few additions and modifications, your home will shine brightly, giving hope to others.

Amusement Is Not the Highest Priority

It is not good to eat much honey; so to seek one's own glory is not glory. Whoever has no rule over his own spirit is like a city broken down, without walls.

Proverbs 25:27–28 (NKJV)

Great!" I thought. "It's time for my show!" Driving home from the mall in my minivan, I turned the radio to *Focus on the Family*. I was a mother of a toddler and a preschooler at the time, and I needed all the help I could get.

It wasn't two seconds before four-year-old Ethan bellowed, "I want music!" I calmly explained he would have to wait until my radio program was over. You can guess what happened next. He started crying and screaming, "No! I want music! You *can't* listen to talking, Mommy!" The more I drove, the more he screamed.

"Ethan," I said loudly over his crying. "I am not even listening to talking because you are screaming. I am the one who picks what we listen to in the car. If you keep crying, we will listen to talking again tomorrow."

He thought for a moment and then screamed even harder. What would you have done in that moment?

Whether it's demanding music in the car or a video game at home, children are growing increasingly accustomed to being amused. Boredom is the kryptonite of today's screen-driven child. Think about it. Television offers hundreds of channels and exciting choices. Smartphones and tablets have games, games, and more games. Even churches are setting up kid spaces that rival the local amusement park.

The majority of parents have capitulated to their children's cries for constant me-centered amusement. Frankly, we've given in because the alternative takes more effort. But this convenience comes at a very high cost and can negatively impact your child's character for life. It may sound as if I'm exaggerating the problem, but I've become convinced!

YOUR CHILD'S BRAIN ON A ROLLER COASTER

When my daughter Noelle was in fourth grade, we drove to an amusement park two hours away. It was a special mom/daughter date since, at that time, Noelle and I were the only roller-coaster fanatics in the family. To us, the higher and faster the ride, the better! The first coaster twisted this way and that. The next coaster was much bigger. We watched other riders spiral, corkscrew, and turn upside down for two minutes and ten seconds. But when it was our turn, Noelle and I were on this monstrous ride for thirty minutes!

We got stuck. After the ride was over, the restraints wouldn't open. With our stomachs already tumbling from the previous two minutes of massive spin, we sat waiting with our legs dangling and our hearts pounding. Twenty minutes later, the ride operator announced we had to ride *again* to reset the restraints.

Several riders cheered, but Noelle and I looked at each other anxiously. We didn't want to ride again; we wanted off! But ride again we did. This time instead of enjoying the thrill, we simply endeavored not to get sick. When we finally got off, Noelle immediately went to lie down on a bench. The day was over before lunchtime. She felt so sick that I stood in line to ask for a voucher to return another day. Defeated but relieved, we headed back down the freeway to our calm, peaceful, non-moving house.

Kids aren't meant to ride roller coasters all day long without stopping. Their brains don't require or desire constant stimulation. As Gary and I wrote in our book, *Growing Up Social: Raising Relational Kids in a Screen-Driven World*, "Compare the difference between taking a family vacation to Disneyland to living at the theme park for a year. Pleasure *can* be overdone."[1] Today's child doesn't just look forward to a summer trip to Disneyland as yesterday's child did. The modern child yearns for, dare I say expects, a party *every day*.

Unfortunately, too many well-meaning parents stand ready to accommodate the child's fairly insatiable demands for entertainment. From jumping in trampoline parks to giving phones to elementary school students, we've spoiled and treated our little ones on a daily basis. Screen time isn't reserved for special occasions like Friday night movie night with the family. The average American child is looking at screens seven hours per day, and that's not including homework.[2]

Today's child is surrounded by tablets, flat-screen TVs, mobile phones, and computers. When a child watches TV, shops for toys online, or plays a video game, the neurotransmitter dopamine carries a signal of pleasure to the brain. Your daughter feels good while she's watching television. But as children are amused more and more each day, the payoff diminishes. The video game that was awesome last month is now passé. Dr. Archibald Hart and Dr. Sylvia Hart Frejd write in their book, *The Digital Invasion*,

> Many of our Internet behaviors, such as gambling or gaming on the Internet, or even Facebooking, can do as much damage to the pleasure center as any powerful drug. The pleasure center can become so flooded that only the "big" stimulants can get a message to the pleasure center. Little, ordinary pleasures are ignored because they do not have the power to overcome the flooding. . . . What this all means is that the thrills of our digital world, if abused, can be as addicting as any drug and rob you of the simple joys of life.[3]

You would never dream of handing your child drugs or alcohol. Yet most parents hand over a tablet or phone to a child without much thought. Because we depend on them and use them so heavily ourselves, we often fail to understand the addictive nature of screens. In a national study of American youths, psychologists found nearly one in ten of the gamers (8.5 percent) to be addicted, meaning that playing video games was causing damage in their lives.[4] Young people today are flunking out of college because instead of going to class, they are playing video games in their dorm rooms. Adam Alter writes in his book *Irresistible: The Rise of Addictive Technology and the Business of Keeping Us Hooked*, once a cucumber has become pickled, it can never go back to being a cucumber. In other words, if your child's brain gets hooked on video games, he or she will always battle those addictions.[5]

When Steve Jobs unveiled the iPad in January 2010, he touted it as an extraordinary way to browse the web, listen to music, look at photos, play games, and navigate thousands of apps. He encouraged everyone to get an iPad, but get this: he didn't let his own kids use the device! When interviewed by the *New York Times* later that year, he said his children had never used the iPad.[6] I believe he limited technology use in his own home because he understood firsthand the addictive danger of having an iPad readily and constantly available. The pickled brain can't go back to being a cucumber.

What kind of society will the screen-driven children of today create tomorrow? I'm afraid what Neil Postman predicted in *Amusing Ourselves to Death: Public Discourse in the Age of Show Business* has already come to pass. In the 1980s, he wrote, "Americans no longer talk to each other, they entertain each other. They do not exchange ideas, they exchange images. They do not argue with propositions; they argue with good looks, celebrities, and commercials."[7]

Doesn't *that* sound familiar? You see the negative effects on our culture when we exalt entertainment over reason and character. So why do we as parents tolerate—and sometimes fuel—our children's love affair with technology and entertainment? Let's be honest. We fall into the amusement trap because it keeps our children quiet and out of the way. It gives us time to make dinner, to have an uninterrupted conversation with our spouse, to catch up on email, or to watch our favorite show. You see screens popping up in restaurants now, not just being held by the customers, but bolted to the tables. I've heard many parents voice their approval because as their kids play with the screen provided on the table, it gives them time to talk.

Cue the roller coaster. But wait. Is it healthy for kids to be entertained all the time? Kids ride from one wave of excitement to the next. Classrooms are providing iPads to improve learning. Minivans are movie theaters. Restaurants are "eat and play" spaces. Most homes in America have five to ten screens to choose from.[8] Remember the principle from Proverbs? Too much honey is not good for any of us. Constant mental candy will stunt our children's growth.

And screen time can mean exposure to content that you would

never have chosen to bring into your family. It's hard to know what exactly a child is watching on her phone or tablet. Content is often violent, inappropriate, and completely at odds with our values. Our children aren't likely to commit a crime after hours of playing violent video games, but do we really want them spending time pretending to punch, shoot, stab, or club opponents?

Parents, we must rise!

In this increasingly screen-driven world, your child's brain is being rewired by the internet. The instant gratification of text messaging, Google searches, and Amazon products arriving the next day is training your child to expect quick answers to life's questions. But that's not how real life works. Dr. Kathy Koch, author of *Screens and Teens*, encourages us to hold down the off button.

> There is abundant research that reveals when we are quiet and really thinking about nothing, important thoughts often rise to the surface. If kids are always trying to fill every waking moment with something, they may never get comfortable with their own thoughts. They might not be able to handle loneliness and being alone, which are not the same. They may have a hard time hearing the inner prompting of the Holy Spirit if they are constantly being entertained.[9]

Your child's brain doesn't function best with a constant drip of dopamine. Get your kids off the roller coaster. Providing amusement for your child should not be a main part of your job description. Make a radical commitment instead: *I will not allow my child to be addicted to any device while they are living under my roof.*

I will not allow my child to be addicted to any device while they are living under my roof.

FUN SCREEN-FREE ACTIVITIES FOR KIDS

NERF GUN ARCADE GAMES: Buy a few helium balloons from the dollar store. Arrange them in varying heights and begin target practice. It's fun for boys, girls, and parents too. Don't like nerf guns? Set up plastic cups on the floor or on a table, and shoot rubber bands at them to knock them down.

PING-PONG AND OTHER GAMES: My parents bought a ping-pong table for their backyard, and it really has added a fun element. My kids love playing ping-pong with their grandparents (and occasionally beating them). We bought an inexpensive set that converts your dining room table into a ping-pong table just by placing the net across. Have items like footballs, Frisbees, hula hoops, basketballs, and soccer balls easily accessible so your kids will go outside and play more often.

READ ALOUD AS A FAMILY: As your kids get old enough, it's fun to switch the roles and have the kids read to the parents. You can also use books such as The Chronicles of Narnia and take turns reading aloud, adding drama with your voice for more laughs and excitement.

KID THEATER: Have your children choose a story from the Bible and give them permission to find props throughout the house. For younger kids, you can provide a simple script, but allow older kids to make up their own. After they practice, they can present their masterpiece to the adults after dinner. This is something fun to do when you have other kids over to play. The more the merrier in terms of roles cast, and it's a great way to share the Bible with friends.

GOOD OLD-FASHIONED FREE TIME: When your kids aren't directed to a particular activity, they will come up with the most creative and unexpected things to do themselves. I've watched my daughters make up dance routines using swing music and umbrellas, teach their imaginary students math, and set up elaborate weddings with all their stuffed animals attending.

THE GOOD STUFF IS NOT NECESSARILY AMUSING

Have you seen any dancing broccoli on television lately? Vegetables don't have the same curb appeal as a bag of crunchy chips or a mouth-watering chocolate bar. As Erma Bombeck said, "In general my children refuse to eat anything that hasn't danced on television."[10] Broccoli may not be amusing in any way, but that's not an excuse to dismiss its importance. Your kids need to be introduced to broccoli (or another green relative). What's the good stuff your child is missing when amusement is pursued as the highest priority? Although this list could be quite extensive, let's focus on two big ones: language development and self-control.

How to Foster a Love for Reading

Parents, educators, and researchers agree language development is fundamental for all areas of learning in your child's life. Your child's reading level will predict future school success. The larger your child's vocabulary, the more he or she will be able to consider big ideas, understand the Bible, and enjoy a successful career.

So how can you help your child excel in language development?

Thank goodness it's not rocket science; it can be as simple as talking and listening to your children over dinner. Researchers found that dinnertime conversation boosts vocabulary for young children even more than reading aloud to them.[11] Think of the word power of combining daily mealtime conversations with reading books. Make trips to the library a part of your family's routine. Create a desire for learning by modeling reading yourself (you might even let your child catch you reading this book today).

When it comes to free time, think books first, TV second. One study found when readers are transported into the emotional lives of books' characters, they grow more empathetic in real life.[12] Reading requires intellectual and imaginative involvement and ability. Television requires only passive involvement. In order to read a book, your child has to focus and develop competency to understand the words on the page. To watch TV, all your child has to do is look at the screen and take a seat.

Yet with all the proven advantages reading produces, children are spending

Helping your child excel in language development can be as simple as talking and listening to your children over dinner.

far more time being entertained by a screen than by a book. Four out of ten families with infants and young children have a television on at least six hours each day.[13] There is a correlation between increased screen time and a reported decline of reading books aloud to young children. Between the years 1993 and 2007, the percentage of preschoolers who were read to every day by a family member changed very little (53 percent in 1993 and 55 percent in 2007). But in 2012 (post iPad), the percentage dropped significantly to 44 percent. That means that 66 percent of children ages three to five were not listening to a grown-up read at least seven times per week.[14] Between 2005 and 2012, the number of children with speech difficulties leapt 70 percent in the United Kingdom. The study blamed the growing use of screen-based gadgets as convenient "babysitters" and a trend for hardworking parents to spend less time with their children.[15]

As you may guess, research shows young children whose parents read to them regularly experience multiple benefits such as a boost in literacy, social emotional growth, and a likelihood of later overall school success.[16] I speak to several MOPS (Mothers of Preschoolers) groups, and the following scene has been repeated again and again. A well-meaning mom will come up to me with a preschooler, a toddler, and a confession. "I used to read at bedtime to my preschooler, but one night I was busy, and my preschooler just read the tablet then went to sleep. A few days later, it happened again. Slowly I got out of the habit of reading at nighttime because it was so much easier to have the tablet do it."

So what if your child reads to himself on an electronic tablet? Will he still enjoy the multiple benefits of reading? Although reading on a Kindle is better for language development than playing a video game, it may not equal the benefits of reading on paper. A 2014 study found that readers who used Kindles were less competent in recalling the plot and events in the book than those who used paperbacks.[17] Psychologist Erik Wastlund at Sweden's Karlstad University found students learned better when reading on paper. Wastlund followed up that study by presenting students a choice of on-screen document formats. He discovered the most influential factor was whether they could see pages in their entirety. When they had to scroll, it distracted their attention away from the story and "took a lot of mental resources that could have been spent comprehending the text instead," reported Wastlund.[18]

Paper also provides the advantage of holding a physical book you can see, touch, write in, and even smell. That's a richer sensory experience. You can tell how many pages you have left in the book, which gives you a sense of orientation and achievement. You can recall where in the book you saw a particular story or quote you liked. For shorter texts, reading from a book or an e-reader is more similar according to researchers.[19] But if you want your child to be able to read long texts requiring sustained concentration, paper still reigns.

My thirteen-year-old son, Ethan, has devoured books like *New York Times* bestseller *Boys in the Boat* by Daniel James Brown and David McCullough's *1776*. He hasn't asked me to read to him in years, but when he was younger, I read aloud to him every night. I don't regret one minute I spent reading with my son. When you read with your young child, you strengthen your emotional bond and the love of reading in both of you.

Maybe you're thinking, "My child is too old for bedtime stories or too accustomed to TV and video games to pick up a book. Is it too late?" If you will commit to make reading a priority in your home, you will find a way. You might imitate the program D.E.A.R., which stands for "Drop Everything and Read!" It's a national month-long celebration of reading that libraries, schools, and bookstores share. You can create your own D.E.A.R. program at home complete with rewards at the end of the month for reading. What subjects do your kids like? Whether they like history, how to build stuff, friendships, humor, or animals, you'll be able to find something interesting with the help of a librarian or an online review site.

When you read with your child, you strengthen your emotional bond and the love of reading in both of you.

In order for your child to succeed as a reader, he or she needs:

Competency

Positive expectations and experiences

An environment conducive to reading

Your child's education isn't the primary responsibility of a teacher or school. It's yours as a parent. No one will care about your child's progress more than you do. If you see your child lagging in reading and writing, take immediate action. Sit right next to your child and read together over the weekend. In my household, Saturday mornings aren't reserved for cartoons as they were in my childhood. Saturdays are synonymous with one hour of family academy. Each child has a book to read and a set of index cards. When they get to a word they do not know, they look up the definition and write it on the index card. We pipe in classical music and for one hour each week, our home is magically transformed into a place of higher education. Afterward, we all turn silly again.

No one will care about your child's progress more than you do.

Even though we laugh a lot, our family's priority is not amusement. We don't make parenting decisions based on the fun factor. On the contrary, we welcome boredom (writing out definitions of words on index cards is, well, boring). If children must be entertained in order to be educated, they will enter the workforce at a disadvantage. Kids must first learn to put in the hard work, *then* the amusement can begin. This leads us to the next big thing your child needs in addition to reading well.

The Building Block of Self-Control

It's our job as parents not to amuse, but sometimes to do just the opposite so our children can learn self-control. For example, when your child throws a tantrum in the store, that's not the time to give in and buy the candy to stop the crying. It's time to leave the store and serve vegetables for the rest of the day. Self-control doesn't come naturally to kids (or adults). It must be taught and practiced over and over.

Believe me, I realize it takes a lot of parental self-control not to give in when you're tired. In that moment, it feels so much easier just to stop the whining or crying! If the thought of standing firm seems very difficult to you right now, take heart. As you practice this discipline your-

We don't make parenting decisions based on the fun factor.

self, you strengthen your parenting "muscle," and it will get easier with practice.

Your child needs to develop a similar muscle of self-control that says, "I'm going to do the right thing even if I don't feel like it. If I don't do the right thing, something will happen I don't like." Don't get hung up because you feel bad when you reprimand your children. The truth is that life will punish the foolish child who lacks self-control, which is far more exacting than loving discipline in your home. Proverbs 25:28 says a person who lacks self-control is like a city breached, unprotected, without walls. There's no protection from danger and enslavement to sin for your child when self-control is missing.

It takes self-control for your child to finish homework before playing. It takes self-control to get along with others at school, learn an instrument, eat properly at the table, or memorize times tables. Self-control, which is the ability to control one's emotions and behavior, is a crucial building block to your child's success.

DIGITALLY SPEAKING

Perhaps you've uttered these words in frustration, "It's time to stop playing that game!" or "You are losing your iPad for the rest of the day!" Technology and self-control can certainly be at odds. I used to think technology was neutral and the problem lay only in how we used it. But the more I read, the more I conclude the technology we use is not neutral. Brilliant and business-minded tech giants are striving to design irresistible technologies. Popular websites, social media sites, and video games translate into serious dollars. In 2013, *Grand Theft Auto 5* made $800 million in its first day.[20] The entire video game industry that same year earned $66 billion—yes, *billion*![21] *World of Warcraft* has grossed more than ten billion dollars, and more than a quarter of a million people have taken the free online World of Warcraft Addiction Test.[22]

What makes video games so highly addictive? First, playing these games brings a strong sense of achievement and mission. Winning is unpredictable, so you keep playing to move up to the next level. Designed with motivational elements such as badges and leaderboards, the games let the player earn points and receive special recognition. Visually, players are taken into another world, being totally immersed in the game. There's a strong social component of playing with others in MMO (Massively Multiplayer Online) games. It has been estimated the average young person will spend 10,000 hours gaming by the time they reach age twenty-one. That statistic should take your breath away. Let's say your child plays video games from age six to age twenty-one: that would equal about thirteen hours of video gaming per week. You can see how that 10,000 hours could rack up. To give you a comparison for that 10,000 hours of gaming, 10,080 hours is the amount of time an American child with perfect attendance spends in school from fifth to twelfth grade.[23]

Girls are also at risk for video game addiction, but as they get older, social media takes over. When your child posts a photo, an instantaneous "like" reinforces the action and invites her to check throughout the day for new likes. Various rewards like messages, likes, and new friend requests don't appear on a schedule, so our kids check in compulsively for that dopamine prize.

In 2012, Netflix introduced "post-play," which meant once one episode ended, the next episode in the series automatically loaded and began playing five seconds later. You can imagine how irresistible it became for our kids to watch "just one more episode," especially if a cliffhanger was involved.[24]

Former Google employee and Stanford graduate Tristan Harris is calling for a revival of conscience in Silicon Valley, asking designers to stop exploiting people's vulnerabilities. About having self-control, he said, "You could say that it's my responsibility . . . but that's not acknowledging that there's a thousand people on the other side of the screen whose job is to break down whatever responsibility I can maintain."[25] Let that sink in. When your child is playing a video game or scrolling through social media, imagine a thousand people on the other side of that screen who have worked long hours to engineer that experience to be as addicting as possible. That, my friend, is not a fair fight. That's why children need parents to step in and intervene with screen-related boundaries, such as collecting all devices at night.

SPIRITUALLY SPEAKING

When the apostle Paul shared about faith in Christ to the governor Felix and his wife, Drusilla, the Bible says Paul talked about "righteousness, self-control and the judgment to come" (Acts 24:25). Self-control is evidently very important. We know it is part of the fruit of the Spirit.

Neil Postman wrote, "I believe I am not mistaken in saying that Christianity is a demanding and serious religion. When it is delivered as easy and amusing, it is another kind of religion altogether."[26] Of course there's room for funny skits for kids and catchy worship songs. But faith in Christ should not be presented as entertainment all the time. A shallow faith in God will disappear when life gets tough.

The ways of God are not always entertaining or amusing, but they bring everlasting life and true joy. A steady stream of cute videos, cartoons, and video games may amuse and occupy your child, but they don't cultivate character or yield lasting fruit. You can be easy on your children now by entertaining them, but later life will be hard on them. Or you can be tough on your children by providing for their needs but not catering to their wants, and then their lives as adults will be much easier.

The ways of God are not always entertaining or amusing, but they bring everlasting life and true joy.

I began this chapter by telling you about Ethan ranting and raving about wanting music in the car instead of listening to my radio program. Did I give in to his screaming? Let's just say we listened to a lot of talk radio that week. I learned a lot—and so did he.

Parents Rising Question

Can your children amuse themselves for long periods of time without a screen? How might you help them practice this important skill?

Parents Rising Prayer

Lord, show me what to do with the devices in our home. I dedicate our phones, computers, tablets, and screens for Your use. Help my family not to waste time with unhealthy amusement. Empower me to lead my children to do what is right and to possess self-control. In Jesus' name, amen.

Parents Rising Action Step

Make it your family policy to collect all phones, iPads, and devices at night, out of your children's bedrooms. Do this for your teenagers also (you might want to charge your phone outside of your bedroom too).

Parents Call the Shots

*Honor your father and your mother, so that you may
live long in the land the LORD your God is giving you.*

Exodus 20:12

The little girl crumpled like a rag doll on the floor. "I want to leave right now!" she screamed loudly enough for everyone in the gift shop to hear. Her mother looked helpless and embarrassed. She knelt beside her little girl and spoke in a soft, reassuring voice. "Mommy's going to buy you a present. Isn't that a good idea? Wouldn't you like to have a present? Just wait a minute, and Mommy will get it for you."

We've all been there—in a public place with a crying child. I wanted to kneel by that exasperated mom and whisper, "Just go ahead and leave without buying the present. After all, that's what your daughter is asking you to do. She should not get a present after she has made a scene."

A few days later, I was in line at a store. A mother with two young children stood in front of me. The smell of the popcorn wafted through the front of the store, causing the kids suddenly to crave buttery popcorn. The little boy and girl turned on the charm, and who could blame them? But when their mother said no, they redoubled their efforts and turned mean. "I want popcorn! Give us popcorn! I'm so hungry. Get us popcorn!" They stomped, whined, flopped, cried, bargained, and begged for popcorn. I silently prayed the mom would keep her resolve.

But, alas, as I paid for my items, I glanced to the side. Those conniving cherubs were each holding a bag of popcorn.

Why do we as parents tolerate and reward bad behavior? The sobering reality is when we give in to our children's demands, we are guaranteeing a repeat performance. An encore in a Broadway play is great, but endless encores of whining, crying, and manipulating are enough to make a parent crazy. Kids will continue repeating negative behaviors if we tolerate them.

Parents, we must rise.

The family stands at a crossroads. We have a crisis in leadership. The problem is not our children, it is us. It's much easier to blame the teacher, the school system, the government, the economy, the naughty friend, video games, peer pressure, or negative TV for our children's shortcomings. But the truth of the matter is *we* have the most power to shape our children's development. Rather than sink under the blame (It's my fault!), try to find the hope in this. This is something within our power of influence. Our children's development can be shaped, and we're the ones who can do it!

We have the most power to shape our children's development.

Perhaps the parents of yesteryear were too strict. Some didn't express love in words. They didn't cuddle or coddle. Kids were seen but not heard. The adult was large, and the child was small. But the pendulum has swung to the opposite extreme. We hover over our children because they are the center of our lives. We're constantly singing their praises and protecting their fragile self-esteem. Kids' music fills the minivan, and favorite cartoons and video games dominate the screens. Kids are calling the shots, and parents are taking the orders. Too often the child is large, and the adult is small.

A clarion-call message for our children: *We are your parents. We love you. We are in charge.*

Somewhere in between yesterday and today is the right balance. Now more than ever, for the sake of the next generation, it's time to seek that balance and send a clarion call to our children: *We are your parents. We love you. We are in charge.*

PUT THIS ON YOUR T-SHIRT

My husband, James, who works as a Realtor, checked in with a client to see how their unpacking was going. Boxes were everywhere, and obviously many hours of hard work lay ahead. Garbage was piling up in a corner of the kitchen. There were three children in the family, elementary and high school age. To James's surprise, they were not helping at all. They were sitting comfortably playing video games. One boy wore a T-shirt that read, "I Put the *Me* in Awesome."

The bar for awesome must have been set pretty low when he got dressed, because he was acting anything but awesome. Popular psychology has trained us to value self-esteem and to nurture kids who declare, "Look at me, I'm awesome!" regardless of how they are acting. The child's worth is exalted in big, bold lettering, brazenly written right across the chest. Be aware of what messages your children are wearing (and believing). Shopping for my elementary school girls, I found T-shirts that read:

> *"I Am My Favorite Princess"*
> *"Sorry Not Sorry"*

"Always Go Your Own Way"
"Home Is Where the Wifi Is"

Browsing shirts for my son, I ran across these slogans:

"Only God Can Judge Me"
"There's No Awesome Without Me"
"Wake Me When It's the Weekend"
"I Follow No One"
"This Is What a Rad Bro Looks Like"

You may chalk this up to clever marketing, cute sayings, or harmless positivity. But take a closer look at these slogans. They are based on a huge sense of self and no requirement for achievement. If your child is "awesome, powerful, and rad," why should he or she listen to you? The message for kids is they are the best and they are the bosses! Yet all this flattery has fallen flat. The self-esteem movement has not produced emotionally healthier kids. Indicators of self-esteem have risen consistently since the 1980s among middle-school, high-school, and college students, but rates of anxiety and depression have also risen right alongside.[1]

The number of children on antidepressants has reached an all-time high.[2] American kids are much more likely to be diagnosed with ADHD or bipolar disorder or other psychiatric disorders than they were twenty-five years ago, and they are heavier and less fit. Adult obesity rates have doubled over the past thirty years, but adolescent obesity rates have tripled.[3] Long-term outcome studies suggest that American kids are now less resilient and more fragile than they used to be.[4] Syndicated newspaper columnist and psychologist John Rosemond says, "There's a growing awareness that the problems of American children—delinquency, depression, poor academic achievement—have multiplied with the self-esteem movement." He points out kids have gained a sense of superiority at the expense of motivation and responsibility.[5]

Family physician Leonard Sax urges parents that the American child desperately needs to learn humility. He writes in his book *The Collapse of Parenting,*

> Humility simply means being as interested in other people as you are in yourself. It means that when you meet new people, you try to learn something about *them* before going off on a spiel about how incredible your current project is. . . . The opposite of humility is inflated self-esteem.[6]

With this in mind, better T-shirts for kids might read, "Work in Progress," "Nice to Meet You," or, "I Honor My Father and Mother."

WHAT'S THE BIG DEAL ABOUT HONOR?

If you were to ask your child what it means to honor you, what would she say? Maybe she might picture a special ceremony where you receive a certificate and bright gold star for good parenting. That's not a bad place to start. But honor should not only be reserved for special occasions. In the Ten Commandments, the first four commandments address our vertical relationship with God. The fifth commandment is the pivot point to the remainder of the commandments, which deal with our relationships with people. It reads,

"Honor your father and your mother, so that you may live long in the land the LORD your God is giving you" (Ex. 20:12).

Do you see how this commandment is foundational to all other social relationships and the following five commandments? It's the bedrock of a decent and good society where there is respect for elders and authorities. Your relationship with your children is the basis for their other relationships in life.

The word *honor* derives from a root word meaning "weighty" (in terms of impressiveness or importance). When a child honors a parent, he assigns weight and importance to the words spoken by that parent. He honors the parent with appreciation, compliments, and praise. Children learn there is a loving moral authority to which they are accountable.

The apostle Paul quotes the fifth commandment along with this instruction: "Children, obey your parents in the Lord, for this is right. 'Honor your father and mother'—which is the first commandment with a promise—'so that it may go well with you and that you may enjoy long life on the earth'" (Eph. 6:1–3).

Today it's not unusual for a child to communicate with his actions or words, "You're not the boss of me!" It's common for teenagers to speak disrespectfully to their moms or dads. This is not how God designed the family to function. When the chain of command is broken, so is the home.

Children, obey your parents is not a suggestion. It's a command. It's not just for past generations of families. It's for us. As our three children grow older (Ethan is now a middle schooler), James and I have made a point of saying, "You won't always agree with us, and that's fine. You can tell us your opinion and disagree. But we always insist you are respectful of us."

Disrespect, which is the opposite of honoring, attacks your place of authority in your child's life. Dr. John Townsend writes this in *Boundaries for Teens*:

> Rather than the presence of something, disrespect is actually an absence of something, the absence of honor for someone, for respect conveys honor. You show honor to people by

giving weight to what is weighty about that person: their role in your life, their authority, their care for you. When teens disrespect, they dismiss that honor. Instead, they have contempt for or anger at a person, or they simply ignore the person.[7]

When this breakdown occurs, it impacts the "long life on the earth" the Bible promises to those who honor their father and mother. During an interview with me, John Rosemond explained the connection between the fifth commandment and a healthy society:

> By carrying on family traditions and adhering to fundamental understandings of how a family should operate—when this is multiplied by millions of families—this is how you stabilize, perpetuate, and sustain culture. You live long in the land the Lord God has given you because you respect these traditions and you carry them on. It's so vitally important to the strength of any culture that its child-rearing traditions are perpetuated from one generation to the next. Those child-rearing traditions in the final analysis define the culture.[8]

That is why honor is a very big deal. It ties one generation to the next and unleashes God's favor. When honor of parents flourishes, so does a society. In the same way, when parents are routinely dismissed, ridiculed, and held in contempt (as in many teen sitcoms), civilized culture falters.

STOP ASKING FOR PERMISSION

You may now understand why it's important for your child to honor and obey you, but how are you going to get your boy or girl to actually do it? You must begin with the attitude and belief that you truly have

been chosen by God to lead your children, and that makes you worthy
of honor. Remember the grand scene in *The Lion King* when Mufasa's
voice calls out from the sky to the adult Simba who has lost his way?

**You truly have been
chosen by God to
lead your children,
and that makes you
worthy of honor.**

"Simba, you have forgotten who you are
and so have forgotten me. Look inside
yourself, Simba. You are more than what
you have become. You must take your
place in the Circle of Life. Remember."⁹

Simba was the true king, but he was
hanging out in the jungle, eating bugs
with a meerkat and a warthog! The roles were all wrong. Simba's
leadership potential lay wasted. The Pride Lands were overrun by
hyenas, lack, and chaos as a result of Simba's absence.

Hyenas, lack, and chaos may seem to describe your family room
on some days. But it doesn't have to stay this way. Take your right-
ful place as the leader in your home. Stop asking for your children's
permission or approval. You don't have to ask your child what he
would like to have for dinner, or when he's ready to go to bed, or to
get dressed for school.

If you need the trash taken out, simply say to your child, "Please
take out the trash." Don't turn your instruction into a question like,
"Honey, could you please take out the trash?" because now you've
opened the door for him to reply, "No, I can't." Resist the desire to
give a passionate speech about the virtues of taking out trash. Don't
ask how your child feels about taking out the trash. Just say, "Please
take out the trash." Keep your instructions short and to the point.
Challenge yourself to use fewer words (and to mean them).

Listen to your word choice and tone of voice when you give your
child instructions. Are you asking your child to do something or telling them? There is a big difference. "Are you ready to go?" is different
than "Time to go." I've noticed the tendency to tack "okay?" at the

end of my sentences. I'm working on clipping off that final word so it doesn't sound like I'm asking my kids questions all the time.

You might not tack on "okay," but maybe your voice rises at the end of the sentence. That intonation turns it into a question. You don't have to sound harsh or raise your voice to make your children mind your instructions. Speak steadily with confidence, like a capable, caring coach.

Many of us are afraid to exercise authority with our children because we're afraid of the pushback. Here's a test to see how afraid you might be of your child or of being inconvenienced:

You've poured cereal and milk into your child's bowl for breakfast. She demands toast instead. What do you do?

A) Serve her the cereal
B) Make toast (your girl can really scream, and who's got the time?)
C) Eat the cereal yourself, make toast for her

If you answered B or C, your child has too much power in your relationship. The breakfast table can quickly provide an accurate assessment of who's calling the shots in your home. If your kids are in charge of what is served and you "just can't get them to eat anything healthy," that's a warning sign.

Consider Dr. Leonard Sax's observation:

Over the past three decades, there has been a massive transfer of authority from parents to kids. Along with that transfer of authority has come a change in the valuation of kids' opinions and preferences. In many families, what kids think and what kids like and what kids want now matters as much, or more, than what their parents think and like and want. "Let kids decide" has become a mantra of good parenting . . . these well-intentioned changes have been profoundly harmful to kids.[10]

A few months ago, I went to the pediatrician for my daughter Noelle's annual checkup. My doctor asked, "Is Noelle drinking at least two cups of milk each day?" "No," I admitted. "She doesn't like milk and drinks water instead." I figured since Noelle likes yogurt, has spinach in her smoothie, and eats vegetables at night that her calcium needs were covered. But a quick calculation revealed she was nowhere near her recommended 1,300 milligrams of calcium per day.

I faced a choice. Would I make Noelle start drinking milk even though she didn't like it? If her feelings and preferences were paramount, I would have to ignore the doctor's advice. But if I am the decision maker as the parent, the doctor will be heeded. Noelle heard what the doctor said in the appointment, and we had a conversation about milk afterward. That night, along with her milk-drinking siblings, Noelle was served milk, not water, at dinner.

To her credit, she did not complain, although I'm sure I saw her grimace. The decision to change to milk was clear because it was *my* responsibility as a parent to respond to the doctor's recommendation. Your children don't need you to accommodate their taste buds and whims. They need you to enforce rules that may not feel good but that are ultimately for their good. Do your best to limit your child's influence and opinion and not let it eclipse your judgment as a parent.

FOUR WAYS TO HELP YOUR KIDS OBEY

SET UP CLEAR EXPECTATIONS. Our children can't read our minds, and they don't naturally understand the right way to behave in different situations. Let your children know what to expect when entering a new environment and provide clear, simple instructions about appropriate behavior. A short conversation before going to a Sunday school class, doctor's visit, or friend's home for dinner can stave off many bad behaviors.

PRACTICE, PRACTICE, PRACTICE. When you have a must-have shopping list in hand, you might threaten, "We're going to leave the store if you don't stop crying!" but you know you can't leave. Instead, plan a trip just to train your child good behavior in the store. Keep practicing until you get it right. There's more work in the short term, but in the long run, you'll enjoy going to the store a whole lot more.

USE DRAMA. Kids love stories, so leverage stories to get your point across. Let's suppose you're going to grandma and grandpa's house for a holiday. You can tell one story in which the kids act naughty: demanding food from grandma, yelling and fighting right in front of grandpa, and running through the house. Then act out the opposite—kids who offer to help in the kitchen, who say thank you, and who follow house rules.

PRAY SPECIFICALLY FOR OBEDIENCE. Ask God specifically for your children to develop obedient hearts. Pray Scriptures such as Exodus 20:12, saying, "God, may my child honor us as parents so that they will live long in the land

You give us." Pray your children will choose to do the right
thing today at school and at home.

YOU UNLEASHED

You've probably seen a parent walking through a crowd with a toddler wearing a leash. Tweak that picture and think of a child walking
a *parent* on a leash instead. Preposterous? Sure, but that is how we
behave sometimes. We find ourselves at the beck and call of our children. The children direct where we go, what we eat, what we watch,
and when we sleep. Parents become overqualified servers, cooks,
and chauffeurs.

Dr. Gary Chapman, author of *The 5 Love Languages,* says,

> The Bible is very clear that parents are responsible for the
> rearing of children. We will get help from the school and the
> church, but it's still our responsibility. I think some of the
> key elements are to have clear rules following God's model,
> clear consequences if you break the rule, and consistency in
> applying those consequences. That's the way God treats us,
> and that's the model for parents.[11]

If you're ready to make the switch and call the shots with your
toddler, child, tween, or teen, here are three proven ideas to get you
unleashed and launched into leadership.

Leverage the power of consequences

Create negative consequences that speak loudly and clearly to
your individual children. Natural consequences are best. If your child
yells at you because you won't let her watch another TV program,

the natural consequence would be no TV the next day. When your child disobeys or misbehaves, the consequence should be so swift and decisive your child will think twice before pulling a stunt like that again. Consequences must be enforced, no matter how inconvenient, so your child believes you mean what you say.

Don't be discouraged as you begin these consequences. Realize you may

It takes time, patience, and perseverance, but the authority pattern can be changed.

inadvertently have trained your child to ignore your first (and second and third) warning. It will take time, patience, and perseverance to change this pattern, but it can be done.

Don't count on your children to meet your emotional needs

If you're depending on your children to be your closest confidants and support system, it puts an undue burden on them and subtly hands them the power to manipulate you. If you depend heavily on the approval and love of your kids, you won't want to rock the boat with your kids. You'll let your teen go to the dance against your better judgment because you don't want her to be mad at you. You'll get your eight-year-old that video game so he'll think you're the greatest or lavish you with a hug.

Instead of looking to your children to meet your emotional needs, look to God and other adults. Get yourself emotionally healthy and fed so you have the resources to parent well. You might join a small group for parents at your church or have a monthly dinner date with your spouse or trusted friends of the same sex. Chat with the children's minister at your church, and ask if he or she knows another family you might click with. As John Townsend writes, "Parents can't support their child if they are depending on him to be their support system. So don't look to your teen for support. Reach out for connection elsewhere."[12]

Seek Wisdom

Wisdom isn't easily found on the surface of life. You won't find it in headlines, sitcoms, billboard music charts, or video games. You must mine for it. The Bible says, "If any of you lacks wisdom, you should ask God, who gives generously to all without finding fault, and it will be given to you" (James 1:5). What a great promise from God! Search for wisdom regarding parenting in the Bible and through prayer. Take an older, wiser parent out for coffee and ask for advice. Job 12:12 asks, "Is not wisdom found among the aged? Does not long life bring understanding?" At a friend's church, every middle schooler and high schooler is matched up with an older member of the congregation for mentoring, and many adults of all ages have mentors within the church family. Even if your church doesn't offer formal mentoring programs, don't hesitate to reach out to a pastor and ask for help to find a mentor.

You might even find a mentor in your own family. When Noelle was two, we engaged in the ever-popular battle over naptime. I'd place her into bed. She'd pop out of her room, look for me, hug me, and run back into bed. You may think, "How cute." But it wasn't cute the fifteenth time she did it. I told her to stay in the room and that the door handle was a "no." She nodded her head in agreement, then a few moments later proceeded to grab the "no" door handle and rush out with abandon.

I tried different forms of discipline without much success. I sought wisdom from James, who coached me to keep the mindset to win. It was like the Winston Churchill quote, "Success consists of going from failure to failure without loss of enthusiasm."[13]

The next day I tried again. I took away her doll, then her bear, then her blanket, then her teething ring. We went back and forth, like two boxers in a ring. Then finally, the little boxer fell asleep. After a few days like this, the battle was won. I wrote in my journal on

December 3, 2008, trying to encourage myself to stand firm in my resolve, "There's nothing more important than taking advantage of the parenting moment and showing Noelle I am consistent and that rules are to be followed."

Remember the clarion call. *We are your parents. We love you. We are in charge.* The greater culture hinges on what happens in the microcosm of our homes. Don't be afraid to step up and lead your children. Your decisions won't always be popular with your kids. I feel a kid's T-shirt slogan coming on: "Someday I will thank my parents for being parents."

Parents Rising Question

Who calls the shots in your home, you or your children? What are some ways you can begin to reestablish authority in your parenting?

Parents Rising Prayer

Lord, may my children honor me so they may live long in the land. Give me strength and wisdom to parent my children to the best of my ability. Help me to follow through with what I know is right. Let my children enjoy the sweet fruit of an obedient life. In Jesus' name, amen.

Parents Rising Action Step

Pay attention to the way you give instructions to your children this week. Tell, don't ask. Make your instructions short, and enforce consequences when your children do not obey.

Routine and Boundaries Provide Security

Obey me, and I will be your God and you will be my people. Walk in obedience to all I command you, that it may go well with you.

Jeremiah 7:23

When Lucy was two, she would often be the first one to wake up in the morning. She'd scream from her bed, "MOOOOOM-MMMMMMYYYYY! I want yoooooou!" That was *not* the right morning routine to begin a happy day for anyone. I'd go in her room and tell her to be quiet so the rest of the family could continue sleeping. After several toddler-alarm-clock episodes like this, I realized I needed to help Lucy develop a different morning routine.

In the evening I told Lucy, "Don't yell 'Mommy' in the morning tomorrow. Instead go to the bench in your room where I will leave you a surprise book. Read that book in your bed for a few minutes, and then you can come into my room quietly." The next morning, to my shock and relief, I wasn't awakened by my name piercing the

airwaves. Lucy walked proudly—and quietly—into my room to use
the bathroom. Then she went back into her room. When I peeked in
on her, I couldn't believe my eyes. She was looking through that picture book in her bed. I told her how proud I was of her and thanked
her for being quiet in the morning. Her eyes beamed with pride; she
liked this new routine too.

That night she said, "Put a book on my bench again, Mommy!"
and I did. We were all much happier with the new morning ritual.
I saw firsthand how my daughter thrived with routine and predict-
ability. A schedule helps boys and girls order their young worlds,
making them feel secure. Structure isn't boring, dull, or stifling.
Routines help kids know what comes next and that brings a sense
of comfort and stability. Rhythms you can count on make the world
a friendlier, more manageable place to grow up in. Healthy routines
create confident kids.

In this day of overload and most families feeling far too busy,
what routines will give you the most bang for your parenting buck?

A schedule helps boys and girls order their young worlds, making them feel secure.

Begin with the big two family game
changers: mealtime and bedtime. I'll
talk more about mealtime in chapter
6, so let's tackle bedtime. Healthy
bedtime ingredients include putting
on pajamas, brushing teeth, reading,
on pajamas, brushing teeth, reading,
and praying. When your child knows the drill and has a regular routine, there's little fuss or pushback. The pattern becomes automatic.
Do your best to keep the same bedtime from one day to the next. Of
course there will be exceptions, but for the most part, try to get the
lights out at the same time each evening. These cues facilitate better
sleep and provide a sense of security and love.

Be sure to keep screens out of the bedtime ritual, ideally turning off all screens thirty minutes before bedtime. Sleep expert Dr.

Archibald Hart suggests setting aside priority time for your children's bed-time ritual, say twenty or more min-
Healthy routines create confident kids.

utes each evening consistently. He says, "In these days of stress and work pressures, parents need to give this time the highest priority. Allow your children to tell you about their day or talk about what-ever is on their minds. Find something your children did that day for which you are grateful and tell them so."[1]

STRESS-REDUCING ROUTINES FOR BLENDED FAMILIES

- Give children a little down time when they first arrive to give them time to acclimate.
- Provide a storage space for each child and instruct siblings not to touch others' belongings.
- Expect chores to be done in both households so children are contributing, responsible members of each family.
- Do your best to make screen time rules, chores, homework, and bedtime as similar as possible between the homes.
- Ask the other parent(s), "What is working for you at home?" Be willing to learn from each other and try to implement what works well in both homes.

A LESSON ON BOUNDARIES FROM FLUFFY

While he was growing up, my husband, James, had a poodle named Fluffy, who was trained not to go into the kitchen. Where the kitchen linoleum began, Fluffy's kingdom ended. James figured if his dad could train a dog not to go in the kitchen, certainly he could train our crawling baby Ethan to do the same. James placed a long strip of blue tape on the floor to delineate the kitchen. He looked at Ethan and pointed to the approved side of the tape. "Yes, you can crawl here." Then he pointed to the forbidden kitchen on the other side of the blue tape. "No," he said sternly and gravely. "This is a no."

When Ethan crawled into the kitchen, James placed him back on the other side of the blue tape and said "no" with his booming voice and also in sign language for added emphasis. When Ethan continued to wander over the blue tape, he would be brought back with that stern "no" and a tap to his bottom. There were tears, but Ethan quickly learned to mind that blue line. He learned to play in the approved space next to the kitchen quite happily.

Our friends thought our blue line barrier was crazy and swore it would never work once Ethan started walking. We were (understandably) mocked and even a bit ridiculed. But do you know what happened? Once Ethan started walking, he was so used to the blue line that he stayed out of the kitchen. He'd walk right up to the line and stop on a dime. When he turned four, we grandly announced, "You are now old enough to enter the kitchen."

Crazy James was vindicated! Our son had learned to mind the same boundary his dad's childhood poodle had! It turns out a child *can* learn new tricks. A child needs clear boundaries to explain what is acceptable and what is not. Kids need guardrails and restraints only parents can provide. Do you remember being a teenager and thinking, "If I did *that*, my mom and dad would kill me"? That healthy fear and respect of authority kept you out of trouble. We had positive reinforcement ("Good job doing your homework"), but we also feared negative consequences for misbehavior.

We must not abandon the disciplinary part of parenting in the name of being positive. All praise creates a selfish, unrepentant son or daughter. Remember Ethan crawling in the kitchen and the tap to his bottom when he crossed the blue tape? We first learned that tap from my lactation specialist who advised me to tap him when he bit down during breastfeeding. That tap let him know, "Hey, stop doing that!" and Ethan got the message. Discipline is a way of showing love.

Kids need the guardrails and restraints only parents can provide.

My friend Rose is an enthusiastic and godly grandmother who I look up to. She is convinced that children are crying out for a line to be drawn, a boundary line. She sees the danger of teaching children that family life, or all of life, is all about them. The more kids expect everything to revolve around their wants and needs, the more selfish and unruly they become. She told me that parents show love by not letting their kids become the "gods of the household." It's more than okay for parents to discipline their children.

OFFER A OR B, NOT A THROUGH Z

Consider the cereal aisle and how many colorful boxes children have to choose from to go along with their milk. Did you know there are more than a dozen types of Cheerios alone? These include Banana Nut, Cinnamon Burst, Frosted, Fruity, Multi Grain Dark Chocolate Crunch, and Dulce de Leche. This abundance of delicious and appealing options is catering to a generation of parents who want to give their children more. No more sawdust-tasting cereal for everyone! Jill gets Frosted Cheerios, Jack gets Banana Nut, and Junior gets Cinnamon Burst.

Isn't this plethora of options a positive gain for the family? Not really. When you regularly offer children whatever they want from

A to Z, you unduly create individuals who balk when they don't get their way. Young kids actually need us as parents to restrict their freedom, not expand it. Left on their own, children won't choose vegetables for dinner. They'll eat French fries. They won't read a book. They'll spend money on video games. They won't go to bed on time. They'll stay up and hope you're too busy to notice.

Now it is healthy for a child to make some choices so he or she can practice decision making at home. You can pose options like, "Would you like to do your homework or straighten up your room first?" or, "Would you like to wear your blue dress or your red one to church?" We can help our children develop good habits by imposing boundaries. For instance, before your son can watch television, ask if he has completed his responsibilities first.

Television is definitely a place where you want to have clear boundaries. Which shows are okay to watch? How long can children watch TV on a weekday? On a weekend? When Dr. Gary Chapman's children were growing up, they didn't have iPads or smartphones to contend with, but they did have television. He and his wife chose about five different programs that were fine to watch. The kids were allowed to choose any of those programs to watch, once a day, for thirty minutes. Dr. Chapman says, "We were developing their ability to choose and make decisions, but we were also setting boundaries. Both of those things are important: to teach children how to make decisions and to live within boundaries."[2]

TEACHING YOUR CHILD TO FLEX

I've had the following conversation with my children many times. Can you relate?

"Take a shower."

"I took one yesterday."

"I don't care. Take one again today."

"No way, do I really have to?"

The directions we give our children can fall on deaf ears. But we as parents must enforce boundaries from personal hygiene to how long you can play a video game. Dr. Todd Cartmell, a psychologist and author of *8 Simple Tools for Raising Great Kids*, offers great insight about teaching our children to think flexibly. When a situation occurs your child isn't happy with, it's natural for him or her to think mad thoughts like, "That's not fair!" or, "I never get to play!" When your child has these mad thoughts, he or she often acts disrespectfully and gets into a lot of trouble as a result. On the other hand, if you can train your child to think flexibly with thoughts like, "It's no big deal," you can write a completely different story.

Let's say it's bedtime for your son but he's not really tired. He can either think, "I'm going to flex with it," or, "I'm going to fight against it and throw a fit." Those are the two basic options. Will he think flexible thoughts, or will he think mad thoughts? Dr. Cartmell says,

Any situation you can think of such as bedtime, you can picture a kid throwing a fit, but you can also think there are kids right now going to bed and they're not throwing a fit. How are they doing that? Are they special kids? No, they've just learned in that very same situation, they're thinking flexibly. They probably don't even realize that they are. They're thinking, "Oh, bedtime. It's not a big deal. I have school tomorrow." Notice when they are thinking like that, how much anger is associated with that? None. Precious little. In that state, they are feeling just fine and in that state, it's much easier to make a good choice with your words and actions.

How much trouble is this kid in? Zero. Why? Because he or she is thinking flexibly in a situation that isn't his or her desired thing.[3]

It's not hard to explain to your child this "flexible thoughts versus mad thoughts" concept. You can help your child come up with personalized flexible statements. You can join your child in memorizing these flexibles and using them yourself. Dr. Cartmell continues,

> You want to get flexible thoughts in their heads so they can use them quickly. It's like a light saber. Flexible thoughts aren't powerful because they are positive sounding. They are powerful because they are true. "The sooner you start, the sooner you're done." That's a true statement. If you can't have a cookie right now, it really isn't a big deal. When you're thinking accurately, it helps your feelings to be on the right track. The flexibles beat the mad thoughts.[4]

TOP 5 FLEXIBLE THOUGHTS FOR KIDS

Introduce your children to Dr. Cartmell's suggested responses as they take direction from you, their parents:

> I should just do it.
> It's no big deal.
> It won't take that long.
> The sooner I start, the sooner I'm done.
> It's okay, I can play later.[5]

DRAWING A LINE WITH DATING AND MODESTY

In his book *Aggressive Girls, Clueless Boys*, Dennis Rainey, president and CEO of FamilyLife, warns parents about the upswing of sexually forward girls.[6] It's important to prepare our sons to look for the right kind of girl in a time when tween and teen girls are more flirtatious and available than in past generations.

Since my children are younger, I asked my author friend Dannah Gresh for her advice on setting dating boundaries. She allowed group dating when her kids were around fourteen. These were events that parents dropped off and picked up kids from like a school dance. When they were sixteen, they were allowed to go on group dates like that, but they were also allowed to use their own wheels and pick up a date alone. Dannah and her husband, Bob, discouraged the kids from being in an ongoing dating relationship until they were eighteen. Dannah says,

> Every family is going to be different. I don't think the point is "God's Word says this about dating." . . . The point is that you start to date when you're already an age that the person you're dating could be the person you marry. I don't think at the age of fourteen they are ready to make that kind of decision. I sure wasn't. We explain it to them when they are about eleven, twelve, or thirteen years old. They realize this is how it works in my family.[7]

In Dannah's research, she found one of the top factors in placing a teen girl at most risk for an early sexual debut is appearing older than she really is. The fastest way for a girl to look older is to embrace immodesty in the way she presents herself. As parents, we (rightfully) cringe at short shorts or low-cut tops. But the problem of immodesty is not just about how much flesh is showing. It's also an issue of the heart.

If your daughter's body was created to glorify God, immodesty is first a spiritual problem. First Timothy 2:9–10 says, "I also want the women to dress modestly, with decency and propriety, adorning themselves, not with elaborate hairstyles or gold or pearls or expensive clothes, but with good deeds." We are to clothe ourselves in a way that doesn't draw unnecessary attention to our bodies. We want our girls to be known by what's inside, not by what they are flaunting on the outside.

Dannah suggests talking to your daughter about dressing modestly *before* her body develops into a woman. We don't want to send an accidental message that communicates to your daughter her changing body is bad. Dannah says,

> It's not about the girl's body; it's about the clothes. Keep the focus on the clothes. Sometimes there are skirts that aren't appropriate, sometimes there are shorts that aren't appropriate. It's about the clothes. Use the word *appropriate*. Modesty is such a big concept to wrap your head around, but when we ask, "Is it appropriate?" we mean "Is it okay?" Most girls know it's not appropriate to wear a speedo to perform in a piano recital. You start giving silly examples like that, and it makes sense. You're not going to dress up in your glittery princess costume to visit your friend in the hospital. That's not appropriate. Then it categorizes modesty into a bigger, broader issue.[8]

What if your daughter is already wearing clothing you now realize is not appropriate? Dannah gives this excellent advice:

One of the greatest gifts we can give our children is apologizing when we get something wrong. The humility of just saying, "Hey, we've been buying this or that for your whole life, and I've just recently come to understand how inappropriate that is. I want to ask your forgiveness. It's really my fault. I guess we're going to have to go shopping!" Every girl is going to love you for that.[9]

Your daughters may not embrace their new not-so-short shorts, but that is not a reason to give up or give in. Just like a child must be forced to eat vegetables, do homework, or practice the piano, your child will wear the clothes you provide. Now, as much as possible, allow your daughter to purchase clothes she likes. One guiding principle I really like from Dannah is to say yes to absolutely as much as you can in regard to fashion. If her daughter asked for a miniskirt and she could put leggings underneath, she'd say yes to that. She said yes as much as possible to be flexible, so when she had to say no, her daughters knew it was now their turn to be flexible, as their mom had been. You may think your daughter's clothes are downright ugly, but as long as she's modest and appropriate, give her the freedom to be herself. I've worn shirts that my eight-year-old fashionista Lucy has passionately declared awful and unfit for public display. But I still wear them!

TRUTH-OR-BARE FASHION TEST

I brought Noelle to Dannah Gresh's Secret Keeper Girl Tour. She watched a quirky, funny modesty fashion show to help her think about what outfits measure up when it comes to modesty. Here are a few "Truth or Bare" fashion tests to share with your girl:

TEST 1: RAISE & PRAISE. Stand up straight and raise both arms high in the air. Is this exposing any belly? If so, your mom has permission to poke it! One solution: wear a tank top underneath. Layering is an easy way to solve belly problems.

TEST 2: I SEE LONDON, I SEE FRANCE. Bend over and touch your knees. Have your mom look at your bottom. Can she see the outline of your underpants? Can she see what color they are? Can she see your actual underwear? If your pants are so tight you can see the outlines of your underwear, your pants are too small.

TEST 3: MIRROR IMAGE. If you are wearing shorts, sit down cross-legged. If you're in a skirt, sit in a chair with your legs crossed. What do you see in the mirror? If you see your underwear or lots of thigh, your shorts or skirt are too short!

These "Truth or Bare" fashion tests shift the thinking process to your daughter. If she embraces these tests as a girl, she'll dress more modesty as a teen.

ELI'S WARNING

Eli had what it took to be an exemplary father. As the high priest and judge of ancient Israel, he certainly knew God's laws and practiced obedience to them. He restrained the sin of the nation, yet strangely he failed to restrain the sin in his boys. The Bible tells us the sons of Eli were corrupt. Even though they didn't know the Lord or revere the temple, they were placed in the priestly office. Eli failed to set and enforce appropriate boundaries and godly routines for his sons, Hophni and Phinehas.

When it was time for people to bring their meat offerings,

Hophni and Phinehas would take parts of the offering *before* it was offered instead of afterward. When the people protested to this practice, which went against the laws of God, Eli's sons threatened to take the meat by force if necessary. Their wrongdoing "was very great in the LORD's sight, for they were treating the LORD's offering with contempt" (1 Sam. 2:17). Eventually, the sin of Eli's sons would cost them their lives.

Not only did they defile the sacrifices, they misused their office as priests by sleeping with women. Eli finally speaks against this outrage. He could have pulled them out of the priesthood. He could have rebuked them both as a father and as a high priest. But he only gives them a lecture and asks, "Why do you do such things?"

As a father, Eli could not change the hearts of his sons. That wasn't his responsibility or burden to bear. But he could have restrained them, disciplined them, corrected them, and in so doing, changed the trajectory of their lives and the generations that followed. I imagine Eli wanted to be kind to his sons, giving them the benefit of the doubt, waiting for them to straighten out in time. Maybe he loved them and made excuses for their awful behavior. But this type of false and mistaken kindness often leads to ruin. His sons didn't need their father's indulgence; they needed correction. They needed boundaries.

Just as had been prophesied, Hophni and Phinehas were killed in battle on the same day in the prime of their lives. Eli and his house would be excluded from the privilege of serving as priests ever again. His sons' unchecked, unchallenged disobedience ended their legacy forever. Are you ever afraid to act as the mean parent who lays down the law and enforces consequences? Perhaps the more appropriate fear is being the nice parent who allows destructive behavior to go unchecked.

Parents, we must rise.

Whether you're teaching a toddler to stay on the sidewalk or keeping a teenager away from addiction, you have a very important job to do as the priest of your home. You establish the boundaries between what is right and wrong in your child's life. You build routines that will serve your kids well into adulthood. You don't want to be all about rules, but you don't want to be ice cream and sunshine all day either. As Josh McDowell said so well, "Rules without relationship leads to rebellion."[10] Your children need to know you love them, and that they must abide by house rules. Rules within close relationships leads to secure, radiant kids.

Rules within close relationships lead to secure, radiant kids.

Parents Rising Question

What is one boundary you need to create right now with your children or one that you need to enforce?

Parents Rising Prayer

Lord, may I learn from the lesson of Eli's life. Give me a supernatural awareness of what is happening in my child's life and give me the courage to act when correction is needed. Give me wisdom to establish healthy boundaries and routines in my home from this day forward. In Jesus' name, amen.

Parents Rising Action Step

Renew your commitment to establish and enforce boundaries. Talk with your spouse and children today about any new rules of the household or old rules that need dusting off.

The Bible and Prayer Every Day

These commandments that I give you today are to be on your hearts. Impress them on your children. Talk about them when you sit at home and when you walk along the road, when you lie down and when you get up.

Deuteronomy 6:6–7

Coming back from a prayer event, I felt energized and ready to tackle parenthood. I had stormed heaven on behalf of my kids along with hundreds of like-minded moms and grandmas. When I got home, Noelle immediately launched into a story that gave me goose bumps.

"Mom, something neat happened when you were gone. Lucy hurt her finger, and I prayed for her. She started crying. It was like the Holy Spirit was on her," Noelle said excitedly.

Noelle had never said anything quite like that before. I was intrigued. "Lucy," I asked, "were you crying because your finger hurt or because you felt warm in your heart?"

"Warm in my heart," she said with certainty.

The next day, Lucy mentioned this again. "Mom, I cried when Noelle prayed for me. I was so touched when she prayed for me."

Friends, when we get busy in prayer, God gets busy in the hearts and lives of our children. While God was touching my heart at the church, God was moving in a powerful way within the walls of my home. The more we enter the throne room of grace through prayer, the more we invite God into the messy midst of our families. I love that God used Noelle to pray for Lucy. Prayer and Bible reading shouldn't only happen from a pulpit on church on Sunday. Your kids can watch *you* read your Bible and pray, and even better, they can do it for themselves!

In their book *Sticky Faith: Everyday Ideas to Build Lasting Faith in Your Kids*, Dr. Kara Powell and Dr. Chap Clark share that 40 to 50 percent of kids who graduate from a church or youth group will fail to stick with their faith in college.[1] Before you kick into worry mode, consider this conclusion by Dr. Christian Smith, a sociologist from the University of Notre Dame: "Most teenagers and their parents may not realize it, but a lot of research in the sociology of religion suggests that the most important social influence in shaping young people's religious lives is the religious life modeled and taught to them by their parents."[2]

It is likely you will replicate, at least in part, who you are spiritually in your children. Sometimes that's good news, and sometimes it's bad. None of us is perfect. Nevertheless, we play a monumental role in passing along faith to the next generation of our family. The Jews had a strategy for passing down faith to their children called the Shema, which includes Deuteronomy 6:4–9. If you ask an orthodox Jew today, or during the time of Jesus or Moses, "What is key to

raising a healthy child?" they would answer **Discipleship is a**
from the Shema, to "love the LORD your God **parent's job.**
with all your heart and with all your soul and
with all your strength." The verses that follow in Deuteronomy instruct *parents* to impress faith on their children. Discipleship isn't the
pastor's job. It's not the teacher's job. It's our job.

RETURN TO RIGHTEOUSNESS

According to the American Bible Society, almost nine out of ten
households (87 percent) own a Bible, and the average household
has three.[3] With more than five billion copies sold, the Bible remains
the world's bestseller. But true godliness isn't measured in owning a
Bible. It's about the Bible owning us. Have we surrendered our lives
to obey the commandments within the sixty-six books of the Bible?

If we're not purposeful, the best book ever can sit for days on a
shelf, while the family iPad remains popular and very un-dusty. Does
the Word of God get thirty seconds of your daily attention or more? Dr.
Kathy Koch is concerned about the number of people who admit they
only use a phone app for Bible reading. That's convenient, but does it
lend to thinking deeply and pondering God's Word? Dr. Koch says,

> There are things that aren't going to happen when we use our
> device. We're not going to cross-reference. We treat the Bible
> in a casual way because it's on our play device. It seems like a
> lot of parents aren't keeping the Bible and God in the proper
> place. Pastors and teachers are telling me that children's
> prayers are becoming shorter and more casual. We've got to
> be raising up a generation who knows they can trust God and
> admit their fears and concerns. Are we modeling that? Do
> they see us turn to the Bible for insights and wisdom?[4]

Although they weren't inundated with apps for handheld devices, the ancient nation of Israel also had a spiritual problem. Moses
had instructed parents to teach their children God's commands and
all the miracles to preserve their faith. Joshua continued in this tradition, and so did the generation that followed him. But within a space
of a few decades, the nation of Israel lost faith.

Joshua proclaimed, "As for me and my house, we will serve the
LORD" (Josh. 24:15 NKJV). This commitment faded in Judges to,
"Everyone did what was right in his own eyes" (Judg. 17:6, 21:25
NKJV). What happened in the gap? Parents stopped teaching their
children the story of redemption and miracles. Parents didn't obey
the repeated command to drive out all the Canaanites from the
Promised Land. The bridge of faith between the book of Joshua and
Judges was broken as a result.

Maybe you can relate because your parents didn't teach you
about faith in God either. Without God-fearing leadership to restrain sin, "the children of Israel did evil in the sight of the LORD, and
served the Baals; and they forsook the LORD God of their fathers. . . .
And they were greatly distressed" (Judg. 2:11–12, 15). How did the
monotheistic Israelites make the huge switch to worshiping other
gods? Perhaps it started with a touch of apathy, rationalizations,
and a few choice excuses. They decided to coexist with the pagan
cultures around them instead of driving them out. Judges 1:27 says,
"The Canaanites were determined to dwell in that land" (NKJV). The
Israelites should have fought for their lives, but they decided it would
be easier to have pagan neighbors.

The Israelites tolerated evil and eventually accepted it as normal.
Ultimately, they imitated the evil by serving the Baals, turning their
backs on God. Toleration turned to acceptance, which turned to
imitation. Like the children of Israel, we live in an ungodly, pagan

culture. We can't (and shouldn't) try to drive out unbelievers from our neighborhoods, but we can certainly put a gate at our front door. We can decide what is allowed in the culture of our home and do our best to return to righteousness.

Dr. Gary Chapman says, "We not only live in a multicultural world; we live in a multi-moral generation. People have all sorts of ideas about what is right or wrong. But we are not responsible for whatever others are doing. We are responsible for our own families."[5]

Parents, we must rise.

It's time for parents to take responsibility and stand against evil flooding into our homes. We must rise up in this sense of the definition: *to take up arms* and *to increase in fervor and intensity.*[6] We've been muzzled in our culture because we don't want to offend anyone or be labeled as judgmental. Instead of getting angry when right is called wrong, and wrong is called right, we are silent. We don't want to be known as haters. Hate has very negative connotations. But the Bible hasn't changed, and it says to "hate evil, love good" (Amos 5:15)—not to hate people, but to hate evil.

In Matthew 15:19, Jesus said evil thoughts included murder, adultery, sexual immorality, theft, false testimony, and slander. Many of our children's video games, movies, and music include not only one of these evils, but several of them. For example, the video game *Grand Theft Auto 5* is rated M (Mature) for blood and gore, intense violence, nudity, strong language, strong sexual content, and use of drugs and alcohol. It has sold more than thirty-three million units, nearly two billion dollars of product as of 2014.[7] The average age of first online exposure to pornography is eleven years old. Twelve percent of total websites are pornographic, making it much easier to access porn on purpose or accidentally.[8] These numbers should make you very uncomfortable.

We are long overdue for the return of righteous anger and zeal for God and His ways. Parents, we must stand against evil hurled at our kids and weave the Word of God into the fabric of their souls.

DOES IT PASS THE ABC TEST?

Before your children watch a new program or play a video game, think through this simple ABC test.

- **ATTITUDE:** What kind of attitude does this program or game promote in my child? After my child watches this show or game, what is his or her attitude like?
- **BEHAVIOR:** How does the content encourage my child to behave?
- **CHARACTER:** What character traits are held up and praised? What character traits are devalued?

Teach your children these ABCs so they can learn discernment for themselves as they grow older. If your child finds himself watching an inappropriate movie at a friend's house, talk about how he could respond. He might be honest and say, "I don't think my parents would allow me to watch this," and then call home. Or he might text a code word home as a signal to his parents in order to save face with his friend. This would prompt the parents to call and ask the child to come home for a particular reason.

DEVOTION COMMOTION

Author and speaker Kendra Smiley's three sons are grown. They love Jesus, lead happy families, and have excelled in their careers (one is a dentist, one a veterinarian, and the other an NFL assistant coach). I'd say Kendra and her husband, John, did more than a few things right while raising their children. I asked her how her family used to handle devotions.

> We called it Devotion Commotion, and we did them in the morning. Did the boys sit serenely and offer praise and prayer to our heavenly Father? Nope, not at all! We'd read a Bible verse followed by a story. We'd talk about it, and we'd pray. We tried to adjust it so the story was told in a way they could understand. We would do all this after breakfast. If we had friends over who were waiting to say grace, we'd say, "We're going to cover that as soon as we're done eating!"[9]

I love that they blessed the food *after* the meal. You don't have to follow a cookie-cutter, prescribed, legalistic way to have devotions with your family. Your rituals may be odd to others, and that's okay. You are aiming for the spiritual growth of *your* family, not someone else's. Find out what works during each school year because your schedule and needs will vary. Don't worry about the starts and stops. Just keep beginning again.

When trying to have family devotions, don't worry about the starts and stops. Just keep beginning again.

If you're like me, you'll buy a new family devotional with great fervor and excitement. You'll read it with your children a few times. Life gets busy, and pretty soon the devotional gets left behind. A few weeks go by and you think,

"Whatever happened to that book I bought?" I have been there, friend. I write parenting books because I'm teaching myself! It's an area where I need to improve. One goal I have set for my children is to memorize one verse from every book of the Bible by the time they leave home. My first step was looking at a study Bible for ideas of a good main verse from each book of the Old and New Testament. I typed them out and made a notebook of verses for Ethan, Noelle, and Lucy.

I was consistent at first, introducing one verse per week. But I confess I petered out after Malachi. I'm stuck in Colossians and random review mode. What do I need to do? Begin again. Our memory verse, Galatians 6:9, sums it up perfectly, "Let us not become weary in doing good, for at the proper time we will reap a harvest if we do not give up." We may not complete every devotional book or Bible project, but we must keep coming back to the Word of God, purposefully serving it to our children.

> **We must keep coming back to the Word of God, purposefully serving it to our children.**

I can't think of a better way to begin and end a day than with the Word of God. I have a friend who leaves a children's devotional near the breakfast table so she can read a few verses each morning. My children have grown up with the habit of reading the Bible before bedtime. When they were young, I would read toddler and various storybook Bibles to them. Now that they are older, they read their Bibles on their own. Don't allow your child to begin and end the day on a tablet playing games or watching videos. Those transitional moments are too precious to waste on something mindless or even harmful.

One grandma I know encourages her grandchildren to keep God's Word in their hearts by providing a little cash incentive when the kids recite a whole verse, complete with the reference. Another way to hide God's Word in young minds and hearts is to listen to Scripture songs—Bible verses set to music. The whole family can easily memorize Scripture through song.

CALL TO ME

In my book *31 Days to Becoming a Happy Mom,* I wrote, "Isn't it true when we're faced with a problem, we immediately turn to Google for the answer? While there's nothing wrong with seeking information online, there is something terribly wrong when we turn to Google before we turn to God."[10] We need to ask more of God and less of Google. Your kids will learn how to reach out to God in prayer by hearing you pray out loud. Dr. Kathy Koch asks,

> Do they hear us pray in the moment, or do we just say we'll pray later, so they never hear us pray that prayer? I think one of the best ways to demonstrate your dependence upon God and your love for your kids is when they share a concern, you say, "Let's pray right now." It's very powerful. Our children need to know we are dependent on the God of the Bible. We're not dependent upon our device and the quality of our cell signal.[11]

In addition to praying out loud as needs arise (or simply to praise God throughout the day), you can have appointed times to pray, such as mealtime and bedtime. I wrote down a funny prayer Lucy once prayed aloud when she was five:

Dear God, thank You for this beautiful day. Thank You that we know You and won't go to hell. Goodbye! Goodnight!

She laughed and asked, *"What do we say at the end of the prayer? Oh yeah, Amen."*

It was an unconventional prayer but basically theologically sound, except I suppose we never have to say goodbye to God. We as parents have the responsibility and honor of teaching our kids how to pray. Fern Nichols, founder of Moms in Prayer, says a praying parent has the opportunity to change a child's life. If we are not praying as parents, who will pray for our children? Fern remembers having a mom who prayed at every meal, at bedtime on her knees, and other times during the day.

> We prayed sometimes when we would leave the driveway for God's protection going to the grocery store. She included God in our everyday life by just talking with him. I think a lot of times we take that first step of having our kids ask Jesus into their hearts, but after that we don't say now that God is your Father, guess what? You get to talk to him, anytime, anywhere. He wants to be part of your life through what we call prayer, which is really just talking to your heavenly Father. We have a friend relationship, but there are those times when we have to realize the awesomeness of who our heavenly Father is. Kneeling can show that deeper reverence. It's not that God hears us any clearer if we're on our knees. It's more about our heart attitude, honoring the God who will answer our prayer.[12]

Fern encourages every mom and dad to speak the blessings found in the Word of God over their children every single day. When school is in session, a Moms in Prayer group comes to my home weekly to pray for our children and their schools by name. I don't say this to brag. I share this because, on my own, I don't think I would have the fortitude to keep praying for my kids and their schools year after year. Make an appointment to pray regularly with others, whether through Moms in Prayer, your local church, or with friends or family members. Taking time to pray for your child by name will completely change the spiritual landscape of your home.

Just ask my friend Rose. After she became a Christian, her boys thought God told her everything. The kids in the neighborhood used to play and gather around a fire hydrant right across the street. When they would talk at night, Rose could hear everything they said from her bedroom window. She had prayed, "Lord, make me the best parent I can be. I can't be everywhere where You are, so You're going to have to let me know what is happening with each of my children." That fire hydrant of secret information was a direct answer to Rose's prayer!

THE ALL-IN LIFE

When my daughter Noelle was three, she would exclaim, "I LOVE blueberries!" or, "I LOVE tortellini!" Now at eleven, she *loves* penguins. She draws penguins, buys penguins, has penguin-themed birthday parties, and dreams of penguins. It's obvious by looking in her room or backpack that she really is crazy about that flightless black-and-white bird. In the same way I can spot Noelle's zest for penguins, I wonder if she can tell I love Jesus. Can she see from my life that I'm all in? Does she know I'm not just a casual fan of Jesus, but a die-hard follower?

If you put drops of food coloring into a gallon of water, slowly but surely that dye works its way through all the water. There's not a pocket of water that can remain unchanged. In the same way, following Jesus should penetrate and impact every area of life. We parents are surrounded by little disciples, who are watching us. Whether you have a toddler at your heels or a teen hiding in his bedroom, they are

We parents are surrounded by little disciples, who are watching us. observing you. Your children are checking to see if what you say matches what you do and who you are.

Not only is modeling a Christ-dependent, grace-filled life important, we must also speak up. There are times to correct, teach, train, and coach our children using words. Life-changing truth is both *caught* and *taught*. Both elements are essential. Teach your child the redemption story of the Bible and how God rescued your life. Let your stories of faith whet their appetite to expect their lives to be marked with that same power and lovingkindness.

Like the children of Israel, our children will be tested. When the Israelites forsook God, the Lord stopped fighting for them. He used pagan nations to test Israel to see whether or not they would keep the way of the Lord and walk like their ancestors.

My friend Rose (the one who eavesdropped by the fire hydrant) is a grandmother now. She taught her kids that whenever they faced a test from God, they would either pass it or have to retake it in some way. The kids grew up knowing that the Holy Spirit lived inside of them, so wherever they went, the Holy Spirit went too.

One day, her son came home boasting about finding a ten-dollar bill. She asked if he tried to turn it in. "Mom," he answered, "if I did that, the kids at the counter would just keep it. I might as well keep it!" Rose wasn't very happy with this reasoning and asked the Lord for help. She said, "You're going to have to pass the test someday about integrity and honesty," and left it at that.

About three months later, he came running home exclaiming, "Mom, mom! I passed the test! I passed the test!" Rose thought he was excited about passing a spelling or math test. "No, Mom. I found twenty dollars in the bathroom today, and I knew who it belonged to. I brought it to the office and told them who it belonged to. I passed the test!" When your children face tests and trials, remember these are strengthening exercises so they may discover God's ways for themselves.

GOD IS FOR YOU

Before you start thinking, "I'm not sure I would have passed that test," or, "I sure have a lot to learn about the Bible," let me liberate you with wise words from Fern Nichols: "Don't give into false guilt. How can we do anything about something we've never thought of? That's why reading the Bible and taking care of our relationship with the Lord is so important. We're changed a little bit, from glory to glory. He doesn't expect us to know the whole Bible in one sitting."[13]

Years ago, Lucy was standing in her class line before school. It had been three weeks since kindergarten began, and she understood the drill pretty well. I started a conversation with a mom I'd never met and moved from my normal spot. The next thing I knew, Lucy rushed toward me with big tears in her eyes, hugging me tight.

"Why are you out of line, Lucy? Go back in the line," I said matter-of-factly.

"I thought you were gone!" she gasped. "You weren't standing where you were supposed to be standing!"

My poor kindergartener panicked, thinking I had left her, when I was there the whole time. I had just moved.

Sometimes it can feel as if you are parenting all alone. God seems far away. Maybe that's just because you're looking in the wrong places. Instead of noticing what is deficient in your parenting, notice what is proficient in God! Don't allow condemnation to keep you down. You can confess your sin before God, and He is faithful to forgive you and give you a clean slate for a new day. There is incredible freedom from sin because of the blood of Jesus. As you walk in

As you walk in freedom, you'll show your kids how to do the same. freedom, you'll show your kids how to do the same.

Keep reminding your children of the faithfulness and goodness of God. Be ruthless with sin and merciful toward your kids (and yourself). We face aggressive advances against the family and the gospel. We must rise up for the sake of the generations that follow, determined to join Joshua in saying, "As for me and my household, we will serve the LORD" (Josh. 24:15).

Parents Rising Question

What would your children know about God if all they ever understood came from your lips and your life?

Parents Rising Prayer

Lord, may the Word of God and prayer fill my home in a powerful way. Forgive me when I don't make You the priority. I commit to obeying the commandments in the Bible, for they bring light and life. Help my children and me to pass the tests that come our way today. In Jesus' name, amen.

Parents Rising Action Step

Pray over your children by name at the beginning and ending of each day this week.

Marriage Takes a Front Seat

*A man leaves his father and mother and is united
to his wife, and they become one flesh.*

Genesis 2:24

There he was, sitting smack dab in the middle of our driveway, holding a seven-pound baby who would forever change our lives. James carefully held our firstborn in awe, the picture of a happy new father stepping outside for a little sunshine with his future heir. Later that day when my cousin visited to see the baby for the first time, James proudly glided down the stairs with great fanfare, holding up baby Ethan like Simba in the movie *The Lion King*.

This baby was a big deal.

All babies are, and rightfully so! Overnight they transform two romantic adults into a sleep-deprived team solely dedicated to meeting the needs of a very tiny person who cannot speak. These babies grow into toddlers, becoming more self-sufficient with each passing year. When our third and youngest child, Lucy, was two, she wanted to do things "all myself." She loved sitting in our minivan, attempting to buckle her own seat belt. We finally settled on a workable system: she connected the top part, and I buckled in the bottom.

Whenever I unloaded groceries from the minivan, Lucy would love moving into her big brother's chair, trying unsuccessfully to click in his seat belt. Kids at all ages and stages tend to take over not only the minivan, but the entire house! And what happens to the romantic couple? They make necessary adjustments, adding the title and responsibilities of "parent" to "spouse." But that's when the takeover usually occurs. Being a parent can slowly supersede being a spouse, and trouble can take root. When marriage is thrown in the trunk while the kids are placed front and center, the couple is bound to get lost.

Perhaps this recent conversation with my husband sounds familiar. From across the room I heard James say, "You're just the cutest."

I was in the kitchen with our puppy, Winston.

"You're talking to the dog, aren't you?" I said.

Married people aren't as romantic as dating people. You've got to work at putting deposits into the marriage bank as your kids grow up. A good sense of humor helps too! I was driving home from speaking at a parenting seminar, and Dannah Gresh happened to be on *Focus on the Family*. The host, Jim Daly, asked what Dannah meant by the phrase "reluctant lover." What she said resonated with me: "A reluctant lover in marriage is the one that isn't really willing to go out on a date with her husband when he asks, because she has kids and she doesn't really want to leave them with a babysitter. She's tired. Even when he reaches for her in bed, she rebuffs him. These are signs of a reluctant lover."[1]

These are tough but true words for weary parents. Parenting is hard, consuming, draining work on many days. It takes effort to save energy to invest in your marriage. But I don't want James to think of me as a "reluctant lover." I don't even want to be known as a willing lover. I want to be an eager lover, someone who is keenly interested in my beloved. That's the kind of relationship we promised each other on our wedding day.

We can lose our way after having children, wondering where the wife or husband we once knew has gone. But it doesn't have to be this way. The most successful families aren't headed by two parents; they are led by a husband and wife who love each other above all others.

IT MAY TAKE A SPARK, BUT I'M OUT OF MATCHES

A few years ago, James really outdid himself on Valentine's Day. He bought a dozen beautiful red roses, and tied them together like a trendy top florist. He bought me a jacket he knew I wanted. He cooked dinner for the whole family—stir-fry chicken, not his pizza bagels.

After dinner, he announced the kids were going to my parents' house and we were going out. I assumed we would have dessert at a restaurant, but instead James drove to a park with a pretty view of downtown San Diego. He took out two cups of vanilla ice cream and root beer—I love root beer floats! He proceeded to spread out a blanket and invited me to lie next to him. He started kissing me, which is really not that unreasonable, considering we were married and it was Valentine's Day. But I turned as cold as the root beer floats. All I could think was, "How embarrassing! We probably look like hormone-crazed teens making out behind the bushes!"

James noticed my reluctance and said, "We used to kiss all the time when we were dating, and you didn't seem to mind. You weren't so self-conscious and worried. Now we're married—it should be more okay!" Oh, to be young and in love again! I realized that night I needed to be less self-conscious and more affection-conscious.

Keeping romance alive and well during the child-raising years takes
intentionality (and occasional kissing in a dark park).

It may only take a spark to ignite a flame of passion, but maybe
you don't even remember where you put the matches. Believe it or
not, you can go to the Word of God to
Keeping romance alive find the match to light love between
takes intentionality. you and your spouse again. Scripture
reflects God's complete understanding of romantic and sexual inter-
action in marriage:

- His mouth is sweetness itself; he is altogether lovely. This
  is my beloved, this is my friend. (Song 5:16)
- A loving doe, a graceful deer—may her breasts satisfy
  you always, may you ever be intoxicated with her love.
  (Prov. 5:19)
- The wife's body does not belong only to her. It also belongs
  to her husband. In the same way, the husband's body does
  not belong only to him. It also belongs to his wife. You
  shouldn't stop giving yourselves to each other. (1 Cor.
  7:4–5 NIRV)

One good piece of marital advice we received was, "Never let
the honeymoon end. It's much easier to keep love alive than to try
to revive something that has died." My friend Kendra Smiley, who
has been happily married for more than forty-five years, has literally
done that with her husband, John. Every year, they go on a honeymoon. They call their vacations together "honeymoons." Their three
boys grew up with honeymoon in their vocabulary because mom
and dad kept going on them! What a beautiful way to raise children,
raising them to see that honeymoons are a regular rhythm of married
life, not just a once-in-a-lifetime experience.

This may sound overly pragmatic, but your calendar may be your best ally in creating intimacy in your marriage. When Linda Dillow, coauthor of *Intimate Issues: 21 Questions Christian Women Ask About Sex,* had three children within thirty-eight months, she was tempted to change her name to *Zombie.* Yet she understood she couldn't put her sexual relationship with her husband, Jody, on hold until the kids were grown. She asked the Lord for help.

> I began to write T.S. on my calendar every other day. When Jody saw my calendar, he wondered who T.S. was and why I was spending so much time with this person. Years later he laughed when he learned T.S. was an abbreviation for THINK SEX, my simple yet effective reminder to keep our sexual relationship a priority.[2]

Adapting this idea from Linda Dillow, I create a calendar event for romance and invite my hubby. Let's just say I agree with what marriage counselor Dr. David Clarke says, "Couples with kids that don't schedule sex don't have sex."[3] You must make regular time for physical intimacy, date nights, hobbies, and honeymoons, putting shared events with just your spouse on the calendar.

Make time for intimacy, putting shared events with just your spouse on the calendar.

When Kendra Smiley was in the child-raising phase of life, her husband, John, who was a pilot, traveled quite a bit. She remembers:

> When John would come home, the kids would pile on top of him and want to wrestle. This was fun, but pretty soon he'd announced that it was my turn. The kids were not allowed to interrupt during my special time together with John. It

taught the kids that Mom and Dad were important to each other and needed time together too.

As you take moments in the day to listen to your spouse, whether he or she just got home from a trip or from a day at the office, it paves the way to intimacy.

BE THE RIGHT PERSON

With a swipe of the finger, the modern man or woman can go to an online dating site and find the "perfect match." For many of us, this professional service didn't exist when we got married. It's possible to think *if I had just married a more compatible person, I would be so much happier.* But I like how Charlie Shedd puts it: "Marriage is not so much finding the right person as it is being the right person."[4] Don't focus on what your spouse isn't. Focus instead on something you can control—what kind of spouse are you?

James and I have a friend who has been a family lawyer for more than forty years. I asked, "Is there a common thread in the clients you see who get a divorce?" His answer was simple. "The spouse stopped putting the other person first. They asked, 'How can my spouse serve me?' instead of 'How can I serve my spouse?'"

A woman who read one of my books emailed me this: "I have been happily married to a wonderful man for fifty-four years. I got your book *31 Days to Becoming a Happy Wife* for my girls and myself. I am always wanting to learn more!"

What a difference in perspective. Here is someone with more than half a century of positive marriage experience, and she is still looking for ways to improve her most important relationship! She wants to be an even happier wife to her husband of fifty-four years. By the time James and I have been married fifty-four years, I'll be eighty-two years old. I hope I'll still be picking up marriage books in my eighties to learn just a little bit more and serve my husband better.

If I had to boil down a successful marriage into one sentence, I think it would be, "Each one of you also must love his wife as he loves himself, and the wife must respect her husband" (Eph. 5:33). Let's be honest. There are many teachings out there about husbands needing to love their wives unconditionally. You'll find it more challenging to locate messages and books about wives showing unconditional respect to their husbands. What if the husband is acting irresponsibly? What if he is lazy or mean-spirited? Is she still supposed to respect him then?

Dr. Emerson Eggerichs responds in his book *Love and Respect: The Love She Most Desires; The Respect He Desperately Needs:* "A husband is even called to love a disrespectful wife, and a wife is called to respect an unloving husband. There is no justification for a husband to say, 'I will love my wife *after* she respects me' nor for a wife to say, 'I will respect my husband *after* he loves me.'"[5]

Husbands are called to love wives. Period. Wives are called to respect husbands. Period. You can be the one to take the first step toward your not-so-perfect spouse. Why not make it easier for your spouse to obey this marriage booster from the Bible?

In Job 31, Job's description of his attempts to remain righteous point out several ways to be a respectable man. Here are a few:

- Be faithful to your wife. "I made a covenant with my eyes not to look lustfully at a young woman" (31:1).
- Be honest. "If I have walked with falsehood . . . let God weigh me in honest scales" (31:5–6).
- Be just. "If I have denied justice to any of my servants . . . what will I do when God confronts me?" (31:13–14).

- Be a giver. "If I have kept bread to myself, not sharing it with the fatherless . . . then let my arm fall from the shoulder, let it be broken off at the joint" (v. 17, 22).

Ladies, we can look to Proverbs 31 to find characteristics of a wife who is easy to love. Here are a few:

- Be trustworthy. "Her husband has full confidence in her and lacks nothing of value. She brings him good, not harm, all the days of her life" (31:11–12).
- Be industrious. "She selects wool and flax and works with eager hands . . . she provides food for her family. . . . She considers a field and buys it. . . . She sets about her work vigorously" (31:13–17).
- Be attractive. "She is clothed in fine linen and purple . . . she can laugh at the days to come" (31:22, 25).
- Be wise and kind with your words. "She speaks with wisdom, and faithful instruction is on her tongue" (31:26).

Men, make it your goal to become more respectable to your wife with each passing year. Women, become more lovable. Put away complaining and put each other first. Manage your household well and laugh more.

WHEN YOU'RE A BLENDED FAMILY

Laura Petherbridge, author of *The Smart Stepmom,* says:

> The healthy family is God first, spouse second, child third. But when a death or divorce occurs, the child moves up a notch on that ladder. If you

remarry, the children have to go back to third place. That's a hard transition, and many single parents aren't ready to move their child into that position. I advise single parents not to remarry unless they are ready to put the new spouse in the number two spot. That doesn't mean you don't stick up for your children if your new spouse is treating them poorly. It means you have to be prepared for your marriage to take precedence. That's extremely difficult for a mom to do when the children have been in that number-two spot for any length of time.

Here's a tip most parents don't think about: spend time alone with your biological children after you remarry. It could be breakfast on Saturday mornings or Friday night pizza. This will go a long way in making them feel secure.[6]

A WORD TO SINGLE PARENTS

Speaker and author Janet Thompson says,

I was a single parent for seventeen years. I would encourage you to find a godly person of the same sex who you admire and want to learn from. You're not looking for someone to grandparent your kids, just someone who can pray for you and give you wisdom when you're going through hard times. Look for Christian families who will have you and your kids over, so your kids can experience what a two-parent healthy home looks like. Don't shy

away from couples and families. Your kids will be
hungry to be in relationships when they grow up.
You want them to have good examples.[7]

TEAM US VS. THE LITTLE PEOPLE

I love the title of Ashleigh Slater's marriage book, *Team Us*.[8] Indeed, the strongest marriages have a teamwork mentality, with husband and wife supporting one another and tackling life as a unit. But those very cute and charming little people called children can divide and conquer a couple before breakfast.

Men and women tend to parent differently. Moms usually say something like, "Get off that ledge, Bobby. That's very dangerous. Please be careful!" while dads are saying, "If you're going to jump, you've got to commit! 1–2–3–JUMP!"

When she was in fifth grade, Noelle fractured a bone in her right hand. She wore a cast for several weeks, allowing that broken bone to heal. Instead of going to the doctor to take Noelle's cast off, James wanted to do something a little different. Now keep in mind, both of our fathers are doctors.

"I'm going to use my new oscillating power tool to take Noelle's cast off. I'm going to do it myself," James said, beaming.

"You're going do what?" I asked, a bit terrified.

"I say I'm a genius. You say I'm a fool!" he joked.

Turns out he *was* a genius. He was very careful, and the cast came right off. He basked in power-tool glory, and we saved money and time. Now I wouldn't recommend an at-home procedure like this one for just anyone, but James actually pulled it off. (Please do not try this at home!) From a marriage standpoint, we've got to back up our spouses, even when it goes against how we would normally roll (as long as what our spouse is proposing is legal and not insane or sinful!).

Ethan rides his bike six miles round-trip to school. If I check my weather app, and if there's just a slight chance of rain, I'll offer to drive him. James sends him out the door. Ethan has ridden home a few times in the rain. He didn't get deathly ill or slip. As you may guess, Ethan had a lot of fun. I do my best to shut my mouth when I want to disagree with James in front of the kids. I try to keep thoughts like, "Don't make them bike that hill," or, "Just let them sleep fifteen minutes longer," to myself.

We moms can lord over the children, overriding our husband's instructions (which we call "wishes"). After all, we have a natural maternal gene that makes us think we are automatically more knowledgeable about all things children! But it's a mistake to parent my kids without the great gift of my husband's mind and heart. Although I understand my kids' schedules better than my husband does, he possesses parenting instincts and leadership skills I lack and need.

It's imperative you and your spouse form a united front at all times when seen by the little people. They sniff out weakness. They will approach you separately and get you to contradict each other without even knowing it. That's why it's important to check with your spouse before approving a play date on a Saturday, homework pass, large purchase, or other such request. The honeymooners Kendra and John Smiley always strove for a united front, even if they weren't agreed about a particular issue. They would speak privately during what they called a SAMS meeting: Sunday AM Summit.

In theory your marriage is the priority, but in practice, the kids often come first.

Getting up before the children on Sunday mornings, they discussed the state of their union.[9]

Parents, we must rise.

Consider the people in your home. Does your spouse come first, or do your kids? This gets tricky because in theory your marriage is the priority, but in practice, the kids often come first. We'll burn the candle at both ends to get what our kids need for school, sports, or church. On the other hand, if our spouse needs something, we might say, "Take care of that yourself. I have enough to do!" If we constantly care for the needs of our children but ignore the needs of our spouses, we will find our homes divided and vulnerable to attack.

Notice again what it says in Genesis 2:24: "A man leaves his father and mother and is united to his wife, and they become one flesh." You **Invest now in** don't become one flesh with your son or daugh- **strengthening** ter. Your child isn't supposed to be your BFF. **your marriage.** You're not permanently attached to your kids. In fact, your sons and daughters are designed by their Creator to grow up and leave your home (sniff, sniff), becoming permanently attached to *their* spouses. To whom are you permanently attached? Your spouse! That's why you must invest now in strengthening your marriage. It may be too late to catch up in the empty nest if you've neglected your spouse during the child-raising years.

Before having children, James and I traveled and had crazy adventures—like the time we got completely soaked in torrential rain. He left his tennis shoes on the hotel heater to dry. The heat popped the air bubble, deflating the shoe. Instead of sightseeing the next day, we went sneaker shopping. Sure, James and I will cry when our kids graduate from high school, but then we'll hit the trail toward more adventure. Maybe we'll even go to Disneyland—without the kids.

DEFINING MARRIAGE FOR YOUR CHILDREN

Young people aren't embracing marriage as they did in past generations. According to the Pew Research Center, the share of Americans who are married is at the lowest point since at least 1920. Seventy-two percent of Americans eighteen and older were married in 1960. By 2015, only half were married. Young people are staying single longer. The median age for first marriages is the highest point on record: 29.5 years for men and 27.4 years for women.[10] Young men and women may be delaying marriage because of cohabitation, financial limitations, attending college, or focusing on careers.

Your son or daughter is growing up in a culture that doesn't view marriage as especially relevant or necessary. Even dating is in trouble. The current scene has been dubbed in a *Vanity Fair* article as the "dating apocalypse," since young people in their late teens and early twenties apparently aren't going out as much anymore. They're swiping. Using dating apps, they swipe left until they find someone attractive. A twentysomething male explains that with dating apps, "you're always sort of prowling. You could talk to two or three girls at a bar and pick the best one, or you can swipe a couple hundred people a day—the sample size is so much larger. It's setting up two or three dates a week and, chances are, sleeping with all of them, so you could rack up a hundred girls you've slept with in a year."[11]

In the "dating apocalypse," there are no more long conversations to really get to know one another. No more courting. No more need for a wedding band and vow before making love. Finding someone to have sex with using dating apps is as easy as ordering takeout for dinner. Combine these apps with the availability of porn, and the dating apocalypse is destructive to the future families of a society. Young men and women raised on porn have a broken concept of what normal sex is like.

In stark contrast, think of the way your father or grandfather was raised. He didn't have the technology to offer a hundred easy options for sex. Instead he needed to make something of himself so he could be worthy of a bride. There was a stigma associated with sex outside of marriage. Today the stigma follows the young person who *won't* have sex before marriage. These are challenging times.

When your children reach their twenties, will they be excited about getting married? Will you have taught them and modeled strong reasons to remain a virgin until marriage? As a teenager, I dreamed of meeting Mr. Right and filled journal after journal about this quest of the heart. The way we cherish (or don't cherish) our spouses will shape the homes our children will create. Dr. Gary Chapman says,

> It's good for children to see their parents hugging and kissing each other. It brings security to the child. It gives a child a model of how husbands and wives ought to relate to each other. Normal behavior between a husband and wife in marriage involves physical touch. When parents don't touch in front of the children, it may communicate to the child that touching is not good. And we know that physical touch is one of the five love languages.[12]

If your marriage is healthy and attractive, your sons and daughters will get a head start toward a happy family life for themselves. They'll see the emptiness of the dating app world. We strive as parents to provide our kids head starts in school or sports. Why not give them a head start relationally? Why not teach them married sex protects from sexually transmitted diseases, rejection, and pain? Your son's or daughter's future relationship with a spouse is more important than career or athletic success in the big picture of life.

LOVE GLUE

James and I were playing a board game with the kids. One player is the customer and the other players are salesmen who try to convince the customer their invention is the best. Products are created by combining two word cards. The customer's identity in one particular round happened to be a honeymooner, so Lucy chose to combine the words "love" and "glue."

She said with her seven-year-old voice, "This is Love Glue. You just put it on when you get married, and it sticks to you. You love each other all the days of your life."

She won that round. Who wouldn't want to buy some Love Glue?

You know what? When we say "I do" at the altar, God pours love glue over us. The two become one flesh—until death do we part. The love glue isn't poured over your children and you. There is no one who is **Put marriage in the front seat. Your kids will be just fine in the back.** more important in your life than your spouse—not even your cute baby or sassy teenager. Put marriage in the front seat. Your kids will be just fine in the back.

Parents Rising Question

Do you and your spouse act as a united front? If not, when could you schedule a time to discuss family matters privately when your kids are not listening?

Parents Rising Prayer

Lord, help me to love and respect my spouse every day. Rekindle the tenderness between us. Make us into a model of love and commitment to our children. Help us to laugh more and have fun with each other. Give us wisdom to resolve conflicts, and give us a spirit of unity in our marriage. We ask for godly spouses in the future for our children. In Jesus' name, amen.

Parents Rising Action Step

Kiss your spouse in front of your kids today. Schedule your next date night, and be sure to save time for physical intimacy.

Good Food Served on the Table

You will eat the fruit of your labor; blessings and prosperity will be yours. Your wife will be like a fruitful vine within your house; your children will be like olive shoots around your table. Yes, this will be the blessing for the man who fears the LORD.

Psalm 128:2–4

Y ou might say our first dining table was a test. When James and I were dating, he invited me to help him restore an old table from his parents' attic. Little did I know, this would be the first of many home improvement projects. Thick dust accumulated over many years hid the beauty of the table under a coat of black. I was in love, so the task seemed light. I used his belt sander and wore kneepads, working harder with wood than I ever had before. The table turned out to be lovely. It became our dining room table after we married.

We used that table made with sweat equity and puppy love for many years until we outgrew it, graduating to a larger hand-me-down table. Our last table had faux leather chairs. The leather had started to peel off, eventually leaving little pieces of fabric on your legs if you were wearing shorts—not exactly great for entertaining. "Um, I'm sorry. You have a piece of my chair stuck to the back of your leg." We ended up peeling off all the fabric from one particularly torn chair seat. We'd play musical chairs whenever we had guests, one member of the family discreetly sitting on the bad chair to protect the innocent guests.

We've had a lot of laughs about our unique furniture. But I've come to conclude the quality of your dining room set isn't that important. The people around the table, the food served, the conversation that occurs—those are the things that make a mealtime great. The *New York Times* ran an article, "In a Time of Too Little Time, Dinner is the Time for Family," back in 1990. The data showed the vast majority (80 percent) of Americans with children said on a typical weeknight, they were eating dinner together. Parents reported that eating together provided a peaceful respite from the frenzy of their day and gave the family a sense of being a family.[1] Two decades later, the number of families eating meals together has dropped considerably. Gallup found in 2013 that 53 percent of American families ate dinner together six or seven nights a week.[2]

What about your home? That's the stat that matters most. The regularity of shared mealtimes may reveal the health of your home quicker than any other indicator.

LESS THERAPY, MORE CHICKEN

I was talking with my parents over dinner, and they made a comment that got me thinking. "It used to be that adults went to work, then went home to their families or to a diner with friends to talk about their day. They would tell jokes and share their frustrations and problems. This was daily group therapy." It made me wonder if the average child—and adult for that matter—is missing this vital connection each day. By eating in the minivan, or with the TV or phone front and center, there is not much space for laughter, lamenting, or meaningful conversation. Maybe we'd need less counseling if we had more chicken dinners together. Counseling is important—and often valuable! But I'm simply wondering if people, in general, would need counseling less often if we had more family members to lean on. Instead of paying someone to listen intently, we could listen intently right around the dining table on most days. Wouldn't that have a positive effect in any home?

It's been proven time and again that eating together as a family on a regular basis creates a healthy child. Consider that kids and teenagers who share family dinners three or more times per week:

- Are less likely to be overweight
- Are more likely to eat healthy foods
- Perform better academically
- Are less likely to engage in risky behaviors such as drugs, alcohol, and sexual activity
- Have better relationships with their parents

With each additional dinner, researchers found fewer emotional and behavioral problems, greater emotional well-being, and higher life satisfaction.[3] The more meals together, the better! If the benefits are so great, why don't more parents flock to the dining table with their children? Families cite the lack of time and picky eaters as the main culprits preventing sharing a meal at home more often.[4] It's difficult to eat together when one kid is in soccer, another is in ballet, and a parent is working late at the office.

Don't stop having regular family dinners when your children

Mealtime rituals are important whether you have toddlers or teens, providing an important sense of belonging. become teenagers. That's certainly a temptation as your high schoolers' schedules get packed, and they want, understandably, to spend more time with friends. Studies show teens who have more positive communication with their parents over mealtimes are emotionally healthier and less likely to smoke, drink, and get into trouble in school. Mealtime rituals are important whether you have toddlers or teens, providing a very important sense of belonging to children. If your family is accustomed to eating on the go or separately, start with one weekly family meal and keep adding.

JAMES'S GREEN SMOOTHIE

2 bananas

2 oranges

2 cups spinach

½ cup flaxseed

1 cup frozen fruit like strawberries or grapes

Water and ice to taste

Blend and drink to your health.

NOELLE'S TORTILLA BAKE

This is a recipe my daughter started making for the family when she was ten. I brown the ground beef and assist with lifting the pan to the oven, but she does the rest.

1 lb. ground beef

2 tablespoons taco seasoning

½ cup water

2 (15 ounce) cans black beans, drained

2 (14.5 ounce) cans diced tomatoes, drained

1 ½ cups shredded cheddar cheese

1 package tortillas

Brown ground beef and drain. Add taco seasoning and water, and cook for 5 minutes. Lay 2 tortillas in bottom of 9" x 13" pan. Layer 1/3 ground beef, 1/3 black beans, 1/3 tomatoes, and 1/3 cheddar cheese. Top with 2 more tortillas and repeat layering sequence twice. Bake at 350 degrees for 25 minutes.

MY CHILD WON'T EAT THAT

Wife and mother of three Lisa Lewis is the chief operating officer at First Place 4 Health and author of the cookbook *Healthy Happy Cooking*. She remembers picking berries on top of the hill to make cobbler as a girl: "The best part was being in the kitchen with my mother and grandmother, laughing and cooking the meal. There was love in the kitchen."[5]

Love in the kitchen. Berries picked from the hill. Three generations cooking together. That may sound like an idyllic experience from a time long gone. Present reality is usually dirty dishes in the sink and leftovers in the microwave. But Lisa says you don't have to be covered in flour to bond in the kitchen. Meals can be quick and easy.

You can buy precut vegetables and look for ways to get dinner on the table more quickly. Lisa has this advice:

> Look for recipes with five or six ingredients or less to simplify meal preparation. I think the best thing you can do is cook ahead. On Sunday night, you can make a big batch of soup or marinara sauce, so you always have those things in the freezer. The fettucine alfredo recipe in my cookbook takes fifteen minutes to make. You can't get to the drive through in that time or go pick up takeout in fifteen minutes.
>
> Have your kids help you because when they are involved, they are more likely to try something new. Kids are picky. They are naturally distrustful of new things. Don't be discouraged if you give your child broccoli and he says no way. It takes at least ten times for a kid to try something and accept it. Your child might not eat something now, but they may soon. Be curious about trying new things yourself. I think that's what my mother and grandmother passed along to me.[6]

For a while, Lisa offered her kids a "No-thank-you bite." They could try just one bite of something and then say no thank you. This guaranteed her children would taste something new, but it gave them the assurance they wouldn't have to eat a huge bowlful. Now her children are grown and stock healthy foods like carrots and whole grain bread in their kitchens. Her son Hunter wrote this in the afterword of the cookbook:

> The foods we eat, and the person who prepares them for us, have the capacity to shape who we are as people, both physically and spiritually. The dishes you consume contribute to

the very makeup of your physical health, but also the kind of person you are. I was very blessed to have a mother who was conscientious and compassionate about nurturing both.[7]

What an endorsement! I'd be happy to have my children say something like that about the meals we ate over our table with the faux leather peeling chairs! I think most parents are pretty good at compassion. We cave in to finicky taste buds and weepy eyes, serving foods such as pizza, chicken nuggets, hot dogs, and mac-and-cheese with astounding regularity. We're not as good at the conscientious part. Several years ago, my pediatrician asked me, "How many fistfuls of vegetables are your children eating every day?" *None* didn't seem like the right answer, so I vowed to make some changes.

That evening, I made butternut squash soup, thinking the creamy consistency would fool them (not a vegetable to be seen). Ethan, age five at the time, started crying loudly. "This is all we are having for dinner? You are so mean!" Noelle, age three, joined in the tears of panic. James calmly informed them of their choice. They could eat the soup for dinner or they could eat the soup for breakfast. Nothing else would be served until the soup was eaten.

It wasn't exactly the no-thank-you bite, but it did the trick. Serving fruits, vegetables, and other things created by God is a challenge in this cupcake, cookie, nacho, pizza, soda, feel-good, tastes-yummy world. One out of three kids in America is considered overweight or obese.[8] Seventy-five percent of young Americans are unfit for military service because of poor education, obesity, and physical ailments. "When you get kids who can't do push-ups, pull-ups, or run, this is a fundamental problem not just for the military but for the country," said Curtis Gilroy, the Pentagon's director of accessions policy.[9] Obesity isn't just a problem in the United States. There is not a single country that has seen a decrease in obesity in the last three decades. We're dealing with a worldwide epidemic.[10]

God said in Genesis 1:29, "I give you every seed-bearing plant on the face of the whole earth and every tree that has fruit with seed in it. They will be yours for food." Too many parents have abandoned the delicious and nutritious foods God has made, opting for fast, easy, unhealthy food kids love to eat. I tell my kids, "Your friends may eat a bag of chips and a can of soda every day, but when they turn thirty, that diet is going to hit them like a load of bricks."

Parents, we must rise.

We need to put good, healthy foods in front of our children. Your child needs vitamins, minerals, complex carbohydrates, and protein to provide the building blocks for necessary growth and development. You are creating a human being out of the ingredients you are putting in your kids' lunchboxes and on the dining table. Will your child's body be built by sugary cereal, glazed donuts, and cheeseburgers? Some of you are old enough to know who the cartoon character Popeye is. He was powered by spinach. Now that's a pro-vegetable message you don't see on TV anymore. It's time to imitate Popeye and put some power in your child's nutritional tank today for a disease-free tomorrow. *Insisting* on nutritious foods is ripe for a comeback.

DON'T TALK WITH YOUR MOUTH FULL

Family mealtime is the perfect place to teach your children good manners. *Don't talk with your mouth full. Chew quietly. Will you pass the bread, please? May I have more milk?* The more civilized you act at home, the more civilized your children will act in public. As you know, the opposite is also true. Make your home a training ground so your children know how to act appropriately whether in a corner deli or a four-star hotel for their aunt's wedding reception.

Don't allow phones or iPads at the table, so your kids will be able to sit in a restaurant without a digital pacifier. They will gain the much-needed skill of communication, as nothing kills conversation faster than a head turned down toward a screen. Require your children to help set the table and clean up the dishes. They learn teamwork and responsibility, while enjoying the benefits of being needed and important to the family. Having some skin in the dinner game will make going out to restaurants even more exciting for them.

The many positive benefits of sharing mealtime together largely depend on what you actually do at the meal. If you get together six times a week, but you just gobble up your food while the TV is on in the background, your family won't necessarily connect. If you use dinnertime to fight with your kids about homework or to argue with your spouse, that's not going to work either.

Be mindful of the tone you bring to the dinner table. If you fight with each other, yell, or give each other the silent treatment in front of your kids, this makes children anxious and afraid for the future. Learn how to keep your conflicts private, remaining calm while around the dinner table. Children aren't equipped to hear arguments between parents, empty threats, or stressors about finances. Family mealtime is for connecting and creating joy, not for arguing or adding tension to an already stressful life. Speak kind and uplifting words to each other for "gracious words are a honeycomb, sweet to the soul and healing to the bones" (Prov. 16:24).

Meals are a time to talk about the day and encourage one another. What did your kids enjoy doing? What was challenging? Kids get to talk, but make sure mom and dad share too.

You as parents should also exercise some control over conversations that take a negative turn. You can keep the conversation good-spirited. Of course, siblings will say funny things to each other. Teasing between family members is fine; tearing one another down is not. Knowing when to wrap it up is also important, especially if you have a bunch of talkers at the table. You know when it's time to move the family on to clean up or get on to homework and other activities.

GET THAT CONVERSATION STARTED!

If your family is quiet and you're not sure how to begin, there are many resources available like *101 Conversation Starters for Families* by Dr. Gary Chapman and Ramon Presson. You'll find great questions and prompts such as:

> Name one talent you wish you had.
>
> If you had a magic wand and could change anything in your life right now, what would it be?
>
> What is the best reason you can think of not to use alcohol or drugs?
>
> Talk about a time when it felt good to help someone.[11]

If you are a single parent, your children can become your support system. But kids weren't meant to shoulder the heavy burdens you may be bearing. Don't talk about money problems at the dinner table. Parents need adult friends to confide in, so kids don't become counselors. Keep the little in your children by protecting them emotionally.

SPREAD THE FEAST

You shouldn't celebrate with food every day, but you can certainly plan and anticipate family celebrations with favorite foods. Before we had children, James came home from work holding a box of donuts from one of my favorite shops. Now you have to understand, this store had just opened in our hometown of San Diego (we knew it from living in other states). I jumped up and down with excitement. James knew he had made a critical error. The box was empty! One of his coworkers had brought one dozen delicious donuts to the break room, and James thought it would be funny to bring home the empty box to me. I didn't see the humor. Perhaps to make it up to me, we would go to this donut shop when vacationing with cousins. It became a tradition for several years.

The point? It's best not to eat donuts on a regular basis, but when you do, make it a celebration with loved ones (and never, ever bring an empty box of donuts to your spouse or children!). Another fun tradition has been bringing our kids' birthday lunch in elementary school. If a birthday landed on a weekday during school, I would ask what the child wanted for lunch and bring it with great fanfare.

When Ethan turned nine, I brought him cheese pizza for lunch. Before I left, he said, "I want to give you a kiss," and he kissed my cheek right in front of all his friends. I was touched by that little gesture. Marking milestones with mini feasts creates special memories and bonds between parents and children. You also see a powerful reason to serve nutritious foods on most days, so when the cheese pizza and ice cream cake come out, these are treats. If our children eat pizza and ice cream three days a week, there's nothing very unique about eating them to mark a birthday, winning a tournament, or the last day of school.

My husband works as a Realtor. James recently took and passed his exam to receive his broker's license. All those hours of studying paid off. It was time to celebrate. We picked up two large pizzas, packed salads and fruit from home, and headed to the park for a celebration picnic. It was a fun memory to mark the accomplishment. You see, the meal doesn't have to be fancy or expensive. It just needs to be a little out of the ordinary and celebrated with words of affirmation. As Asheritah Ciuciu, author of *Full: Food, Jesus, and the Battle for Satisfaction,* writes, "Look for reasons to celebrate together around the table. Make a toast. Pop the sparkling grape juice. Set the table with the fine china. Fold the napkins into fancy designs."[12]

Open up your home for celebrations over food. Don't worry if you're not a gourmet chef. My family will certainly attest if I can entertain, anyone can. The world is starving for communion over a table in this fast-food, busy, impersonal world. James and I have made a point over the years to invite people over for dinner. We've actually met people in line at stores and invited them to dinner. One woman was returning diapers, and we struck up a conversation while waiting in the customer service line. Another couple we met in the paint section of a home improvement store (we were looking at swatches too). Those connections were sparked by something we had in common (diapers and painting) and strengthened over shared meals.

When was the last time you were invited over by someone other than a family member for dinner? If you're like most people, it's been awhile. Reach out to others by inviting them to share a table with you. Not only will your guests be extremely blessed by your kindness, your children will see a living model of hospitality. They will think it's normal to serve as a host—and that's a good thing.

Speaking before the U.S. Congress, Mother Teresa said,

> The greatest disease in the West today is not TB or leprosy; it is being unwanted, unloved, and uncared for. We can cure physical diseases with medicine, but the only cure for loneliness, despair, and hopelessness is love. There are many in the world who are dying for a piece of bread, but there're much more dying for a little love.[13]

Make your home a place where love is freely given, first to the honored guests who live there, and second to all who visit. Physical food is necessary, but feeding one's soul is even more important. After feeding five thousand men plus women and children, Jesus declared, "I am the

Make your home a place where love is freely given, to the honored guests who live there and to all who visit.

bread of life. Whoever comes to me will never go hungry, and whoever believes in me will never be thirsty" (John 6:35). Whenever we open our door to entertain guests, or say grace over a family meal, may we recognize and glorify Jesus who truly sustains us. Because of God's gift of daily bread, you can put good food on the table, no matter what your dining room table looks like.

Parents Rising Question

How many meals do you eat together per week as a family? Only count screen-free meals when family members are talking to each other.

Parents Rising Prayer

Lord, thank You for providing daily bread for my family. Help us relate to each other over the dinner table this week. I will choose more nutritious foods to strengthen my children in mind and body. I praise You for all Your blessings that flow into our home. In Jesus' name, amen.

Parents Rising Action Step

Plan your next meal at home with every member of the family. What day? What time? Make it as nutritious as possible and rich in conversation.

Love Is Spelled T-I-M-E

There is a time for everything, and a season for every
activity under the heavens: a time to be born
and a time to die, a time to plant and a time to uproot.

Ecclesiastes 3:1–2

James bolted into the kitchen and blurted out, "Guess what you are going to do?" What he announced would change my life and schedule for the next few years. "You are going to join Blue Dragon Martial Arts!"

"You see," he continued, "if we sign up the kids for martial arts classes, we can go for free. Buy three, get two free!"

This was humorous on numerous levels. We're always looking for a deal. James, the white boy, grew up using chopsticks at Chinese restaurants. I, the Asian girl, grew up using forks like my parents. I am not into kung fu, karate, boxing, kicking, or wrestling. I can barely touch my toes. You could drive a Barbie bus under my legs as I attempt the splits.

Yet a few weeks later, the fantastic five Pellicanes were decked out in matching pants and black T-shirts emblazoned with dragons.

James and I were the only adults in the kids' class. We sat crisscross applesauce as the sensei showcased the roundhouse kick. I was thinking, "What in the world am I doing here? This is so embarrassing."

Next jiu-jitsu class, James trapped my head and arm in a triangle. The triangle choke is a move where the attacker wraps his *legs* around the opponent's neck leaving one arm in this trap while squeezing. Let's just say I was very uncomfortable. I definitely considered quitting. Friday was sparring day. Along with the kids, I put on the chest protection with the giant red target in the center. I faced James and said, "Don't you dare kick me," which was a ridiculous statement, as the point of sparring is to kick each other—and I was wearing a giant red dot.

But as the weeks went by, my embarrassment lessened. I came to think many parents watching the class from the benches secretly wished they too could join their kids. By now I've wrestled for years with Ethan (what kid wouldn't want to sit on his mom and try to tap her out?), sparred with the girls (James and I decided it was better for our marriage not to partner up), and made some hilarious memories along the way.

Please don't mistake my ongoing participation for competence. My roundhouse kick wouldn't send you hurling anywhere. I don't tap out anyone wrestling unless they are a quarter my size. I'm not at the dojo three times a week because I love the sport (I'm so sorry, Sensei, if you are somehow reading this). I am on the mat, sweating in my gear, because I love my family and want to spend time with them.

You certainly don't have to pick up martial arts to bond with your children through bruises. You might play chess, read together, swim, or ride bikes. Zig Ziglar famously said, "To a child love is spelled T-I-M-E." Zig also said, "Lack of direction, not lack of time, is the problem. We all have twenty-four hour days."[1] How will you use your minutes to connect with your kids?

CREATING CONNECTIONS

When I'm holding a paddle for one of my kids to kick, we're literally connecting. The hours we spend in martial arts each week provide our family talking time in the car, a shared activity, and an opportunity to play and laugh together. Sometimes I have to shush *James* in class so he doesn't get our family in trouble! Dr. Kathy Koch encourages parents to play with their kids. She says, "The evidence on what kids learn as they play with adults is so significant. They learn creative flexible thinking. They learn to regulate emotion and persist with a task. The problems parents have with their children might be radically changed if they just played more. The big solutions aren't all that complicated."[2]

Today's child is involved in a myriad of activities, but how many of those activities actually involve you as a parent? Watching your child play sports, dance, or act is certainly good, but it's not the same as doing something together. Remember Kendra Smiley, who calls vacations with her hubby honeymoons? Her family attended a small country church. One Sunday, the pastor announced they were looking to hire someone to clean the church. Kendra and her husband, John, raised their hands. Every Saturday, Kendra, John, and their three young sons cleaned the church together. She found something for the family to do together! Kendra remembers,

One son loved to scrub. He would clean something and we'd say, "Now remember this is where the little old ladies will come and they're going to make a judgment call on whether or not this was done correctly." The bar was really raised. I believe that taught them you don't just get by in the workplace. There's no "This will do." We were enriching our relationships because we were working together. That was so important. Working together, playing together, being there for each other—that's how you enrich your relationship with your child.[3]

The funny thing is that while the Smiley family was cleaning the church, Kendra hired someone to clean their own house! They divided the money from cleaning the church by three and put it in the boys' savings. There was a time cost, financial cost, and physical labor cost for Kendra and John to clean that church with their boys, but it was well worth it in their eyes.

Maybe you're not quite sure what you and your kids could do together. Don't worry; you're not alone. Author and psychologist Dr. Todd Cartmell often hears parents and kids report they don't have much in common. As a result, they don't do much together. He encourages parents to assume interest in whatever their child finds interesting. For instance, one of his boys was really into basketball. Dr. Cartmell didn't spend much time watching NBA games, but he decided to watch the basketball practices. He learned quite a bit about free throw shooting and form. Playing basketball became one of the things he and his son connected over. He combined shooting hoops with talking about topics that were meaningful, making the most of that shared time to give guidance to his son.[4]

One of my friends fondly remembers her mother used to set up scavenger hunts for her and her siblings. They lived in the country. Her mom would spend hours hiding things, leaving clues, and being creative. She also spent time working with her kids, bringing in produce from the garden, and getting their help with canning fruits and vegetables. These shared activities gave them plenty of time to talk.

Connecting with your children in conversation is hugely important so they will be accustomed to sharing their problems, concerns, observations, and joys with you. Whether it's around the dining table, basketball hoop, car, or during a family meeting or devotion, talk about what's important to your family. How do you solve problems? How do you treat people respectfully? Dr. Cartmell says,

> After you've had a whole bunch of these conversations, your child gets used to talking to you about easy topics and big topics, important topics, and thinking together. I've had a bunch of kids tell me something important in my office. I'll ask, "I'm curious. Have you ever mentioned this to your parents?" A lot of times, the answer is no. I'll ask why not? Often they say, "It would be weird to talk to them." The absence of that familiarity of talking has huge implications.[5]

Dr. Cartmell offers two small ways you can connect to your child starting today:

- *Get in the habit of maintaining a regular flow of brief, warm physical touch.* Give your child high fives, squeezes on the shoulders, regular contact on a daily basis. This creates a warm, connected family atmosphere.
- *Have daily check-ins.* Pray together even for a few moments. Check in by asking, "How was your day?" Have a time when each child is the sole focus of your attention, showing them you are interested in the details of their lives.[6]

It's impossible to connect to your kids if you're not spending time with them each day. Playing, laughing, and having fun together can change the atmosphere of your home overnight, providing a catalyst for conversation.

DON'T SQUANDER YOUR PENNIES

Author Eryn Lynum stood with her husband and their two boys onstage at Child Dedication Sunday. The pastor handed the couple a glass jar of exactly 936 shiny copper pennies for their youngest being dedicated. One penny for each week they had to raise their son. Eryn was instructed to remove one penny each week as a visual reminder of how much time they had left before he became an adult. Eryn's book *936 Pennies* chronicles her parenting journey and how that penny jar has changed the way she uses time. Whether or not you received a jar of pennies at a child's dedication ceremony, unless there is a tragedy, you too have the gift of 936 weeks with your child from birth to age eighteen.[7]

Let's say you spend an average of three hours a day with your child on weekdays, and five hours a day on weekends. That would total 23,400 hours spent raising your child, which sounds fairly impressive. But now compare the number of hours the average child is spending on screens each day. If your child is spending seven hours per day watching TV, texting, doing homework, playing video games, or posting social media, that equals 45,864 hours—almost double the time spent with you.

Those totals do not have to reflect your family's story. You can intentionally spend more quality time with your kids, squandering less time on your devices and keeping your children from wasting hour after hour, day after day. Many times, we the parents are the bigger offenders when it comes to wasting time with phones, flat screens, and computers. A study of six thousand children found:

54 percent felt their parents checked their phones too often.
36 percent said their parents' worst habit was getting distracted by their phones in the midst of a conversation.

32 percent said this behavior made them feel unimportant. 56 percent said they would like to confiscate their parents' cellphones.[8]

Many moms like me have picked up blogging, looking up old friends on social media, or following a women's group at church. These activities can be useful, but Dr. Kathy Koch issues this warning:

> I'm not opposed to having a blog or using social media for good, but I think a lot of moms discovered joy in that, and they began to disconnect from their kids, who wanted more mommy time. Let's admit that. Children tell me they very much resent being told to turn off their phone when Dad's is in his belt and Mom's is in her hand. I respect that. I praise God I've been able to work with dads who have stopped checking news, sports, and banking websites while their children are awake. They do that when their children are in bed. I appreciate that they sacrifice a bit of their curiosity to put kids first.
>
> Parents need to engage with their children in social play without anything digital. What if we put board games on the coffee table, a Frisbee and football at the back door, and a jigsaw puzzle on a corner table? We are not anti-tech. What we're concerned about is what is technology doing to the beliefs and behaviors of kids, and what it is doing to the family unit.[9]

Quality time means your child has your undivided attention without having to compete with technology or any other distraction. As of this writing, I have about 260 pennies left to spend with my oldest child, thirteen-year-old Ethan. That brings tears to my eyes—and

Quality time means your child has your undivided attention without having to compete with technology or any other distraction.

you can ask my friends, I'm not a crier. The bulk of my investment—676 pennies representing weeks—has been deposited in the bank of my son's heart.

Parents, we must rise.

These weeks, these gifts of time, are too precious to be squandered.

DIG FOR THE TREASURES

English philosopher Bern Williams once said, "No symphony orchestra ever played music like a two-year-old girl laughing with a puppy."[10] Some moments with your children sound like a symphony. Others sound more like a dozen crazy people banging on drums. We can stumble upon treasured moments with our kids, but usually it takes years of listening to uncover the diamonds.

Did you know your child is similar to a dump truck? No, it's not that they're stinky or caked in dirt. First of all, as Dr. Todd Cartmell explained to me, they get filled up with stuff. All of the things that are important to them fill up their dump truck. Their worries, cares, triumphs, questions, jokes, cafeteria conversations—they're all in there. Dr. Cartmell says they're "dump trucks filled with diamonds."[11]

At some point, the cargo inside becomes so heavy the dump truck has to unload somewhere. When you take the time to listen to your children, you're allowing them to unload the valuable cargo of their dump trucks. Dr. Cartmell explains,

Listening is letting my kids unload their truck. It's going to get filled up again, and it's going to get unloaded again. They are going to learn by experience where the best unloading spots are. Who really cares about what's in my truck? That's where they're going to go back over and over again. I want that best unloading spot to be my wife and me.

How can you make talking to you a valuable experience for your child? Start by listening first and talking second. When the stuff is coming out of the truck, you really are listening. You're not giving advice. When I say it's a bunch of diamonds, I am not joking. You don't want to miss a thing. You want to catch every feeling, every nuance, every detail. You really want to understand it. When you ask clarifying questions and use summary statements to show you are really listening, your child gets the feeling, wow, Mom or Dad is really paying attention. That was really helpful.[12]

One night before bedtime, Noelle was crying a little bit in her bunk bed. I asked her what was wrong, and she said she didn't really know. We talked about the day, and I just listened. By the time we turned off the light and said goodnight, she was okay. Later I told James I used my mom superpowers to cheer Noelle. What I really did was listen, and anyone can use that superpower.

Listening is very important during your children's teen years even if it seems like they don't want to talk, especially about sex. Author Dannah Gresh reminds parents even the most sheltered children are sometimes introduced to sex by their peers before they talk about it with their parents. They have heard the word "sex" and they are wondering what it means. Dannah says,

One of the most-searched words from children on the internet out of curiosity is sex. Before you know it, your child is watching something that would break your spirit. I encourage you to be the first one to introduce the topic because then you get to form their values about sex. It's easier to build a foundation of values from the ground up than to tear something down that's not built correctly. Most child psychologists will advise starting these conversations at about age nine. Many kids are at risk of hearing about it before because of all the media about sex. I would encourage parents to set goals about what age to begin talking about sex, and hold each other accountable because it's easy to let this conversation pass. If you talk to your kids when they are young, they might giggle and laugh, but at least their mind hasn't been warped by the world yet.[13]

I remember when Ethan was in second grade and Noelle was in kindergarten. After breakfast she asked if kids could have babies or if that was just for adults. I told her only women could have babies and that God designed mommies and daddies to have babies. Peppered by more questions, I used the word *sex*, which really got Noelle laughing. She giggled, "Sex, sex, sexaphone [saying it like *saxophone*]." She started howling about this new word and couldn't stop laughing. That ended the conversation, thank goodness, and we picked it back up around fifth grade!

5 LITTLE WAYS TO SPEND
MORE TIME WITH YOUR KIDS

Take one of them out for breakfast once a month. I got this idea from my neighbor who began taking out her high-school-aged daughter for breakfast to talk about books they would read together.

Be there (even when you're not there). Write notes to your children and put them in backpacks, lunchboxes, under pillows, or somewhere else around the house to find. On occasion I'll put a Post-it note in Lucy's lunchbox. To my surprise, she keeps all these tiny notes in the pocket of her lunchbox.

Walk around the block. After dinner, invite one of your kids to walk down the street with you. It will probably take less than ten minutes, but it provides time for undivided attention. Leave your phone at home.

Do errands together. Need to run to the bank? Take one of your children for some one-on-one time. Can't bring just one and leave the rest at home? Bring all the kids and take turns sharing highs and lows of the day during the car ride.

Create a weekend ritual. What's a fun activity you can do most weekends? Maybe it's a board game everyone can play or a bike ride in the neighborhood. Kids can help make pancakes on Saturday mornings, or one night can be family movie night.

CARVE TIME FOR TRAINING

Last year we got our first pet ever: a Goldendoodle puppy named Winston. James created his own "Dog 101" required course. Before bringing our adorable brown puppy home, our family watched about seven hours of dog training videos. We knew having a puppy would be hard work, and we weren't about to leave it to chance. We were willing to invest a lot of time training our puppy, so we could then enjoy a well-behaved dog for many years to come.

The first few weeks with Winston were rough. It was like having a newborn in the house again, waking up at midnight and 4 a.m. to take him out to go potty. Where's "Poop and Scoop" when you need them? By day, Winston ate grass, jumped up to bite us, and did what we called the "buckin' bronco"—running crazily all over the backyard. Each member of our family spent daily time with Winston, putting him on our laps so he would bond with us. Our turning point came when Winston turned fourteen weeks old. We called in the big guns—a professional dog trainer.

The first commands the trainer taught were *wait, come,* and *off*. He taught us the rule of two: say it twice, then help the dog obey. After his first training session, Winston was exhausted. He took a three-hour nap! But the real work began after the trainer left. Now we had to be consistent and follow through on the commands we'd been taught. Training takes time, energy, and commitment. It can be hard to persevere when you have a thousand other things to do. I wrote this in my journal about my puppy, which had remarkable parallels to parenting:

> It's so much easier to let things go. But if we ride him for the first year, he'll be such a good dog for the rest of his life. It's like being tough on a toddler to have a more obedient child. It's not normal to watch your puppy so carefully, looking to correct behavior. You want to give up a few weeks into it. But when the puppy learns, life is better for everyone. Our quality of life with Winston is improving because he's learning "off" for the dishtowels. He doesn't bite our legs anymore. It's like having a different dog.

James has been the most passionate about Winston's training, watching hours of dog-training videos and spending hours with "The

W." Now at one year old, Winston can stay in place on command (lying on a mat, for instance) in our home even when we have a dozen guests in the house. He does great on walks, runs on the curb while James bikes next to him, and waits for our signal to begin eating.

Winston is half golden retriever, so he's very social. You never have to wonder where he is. If we're home, he'll be plopped down at someone's feet. When I walk to the laundry room, he follows me (plus that's where we keep the food). When I go upstairs, he waits at the foot of the stairs until I reappear. He just wants to be close, and that's very endearing.

Winston is still a puppy, but he weighs seventy-five pounds now. His early training was imperative for our safety—he could easily knock any of us down or pounce on my parents to their demise during visits. We've invested hours disciplining and lavishing affection on Winston. You may wonder what my puppy has to do with spending time with your children? Quite a bit actually! If you want a well behaved dog, you must invest time to learn about dogs and to practice what you are learning. Adult dogs can be rehabilitated and trained; they don't have to be puppies to learn.

Children are the same way. They can be trained as toddlers or rehabilitated as teens. It just takes time and effort. As I experienced with my puppy, it's easier just to let things slide. It's a sacrifice to attend parenting seminars, read articles and books, take your children for walks, and save up for special vacations. But I promise the investment of your time and energy is worth it. In the same way we worked with Winston on eating etiquette, walking on a leash, and staying in one place, you can work with your child on the next skills he or she needs to learn. It might be tying shoelaces, apologizing to a friend, or learning to drive. Take time to train your children because, if you won't, who will?

Warren Buffett said, "Someone is sitting in the shade today

because someone planted a tree a long time ago."[14] The time for planting and investing is now.

Speaking of Warren Buffett, James has been teaching Ethan a little bit about the stock market, and Ethan has bought his first stock. One day in the car Ethan said, "People should invest in moms." I asked him why. He answered, "I put money in the stock market, and it went down. But the first time I ate lunch off-campus with the 100 percent club, you gave me five dollars, and the next time, you gave me seven dollars. Now that's a good investment!"

There are certainly times when we parents appear as good investments to our kids. Other times we are liabilities. We too go up and down like the stock market. We won't always get it right. Maybe you haven't been spending as much quality time with your children as you'd like. I love what Henry Ford says: "Failure is simply the opportunity to begin again, this time more intelligently."[15]

You can make changes right now to connect daily with your kids. The Rat Race can wait . . . your work will always be there, but your 936 pennies are counting down.

Parents Rising Question

Would your children say you are a good listener? Do they come to you to unload their dump truck?

Parents Rising Prayer

Lord, thank You for the gift of this day with my family. May I use my time wisely to train my children in Your ways. Help me be a patient listener and mine for diamonds in the words my kids speak. Slow me down so I'm not always in a hurry. May my children feel loved because of the time I spend with them. In Jesus' name, amen.

Parents Rising Action Step

Ask your child, "Do you think I spend enough time with you?" If you have more than one child, talk to each child separately about this. Listen to their answers with an open mind. If they answer "no," talk about ways you might spend more time together in the next week.

Launching Adults, Not Babying Children

Don't let anyone look down on you because you
are young, but set an example for the believers
in speech, in conduct, in love, in faith and in purity.

1 Timothy 4:12

A bout ten weeks after Ethan was born, James kicked me out of the house at 6:15 a.m. to attend a neighborhood cycling class. I was barely awake, but I knew it would be good for me. Thirteen years later, I still fill up my water bottle and meet my mom for cycling class. Just this morning, I struggled to keep up. My muscles ached. I wanted to stop. But my instructor kept yelling, "You're already here! You might as well work! Stop swinging your hips! More tension on the bike!"

I had a good workout because the instructor pushed me to try despite my feelings. She egged me on when I wanted to quit. She wasn't trying to make me miserable; on the contrary, her goal is to make me strong. Imagine if she said one morning, "Arlene, you look tired. Why don't you just skip class and go out to coffee instead?" Awesome! I'd be sipping a vanilla latte instead of sweating. But I don't need a trainer who babies me. I need someone to keep me in line to make me stronger. That's the role of the instructor.

Many children today could use a wise instructor instead of a compassionate buddy. Kids are being babied when they should be pushed. Please don't misunderstand. I'm not saying your first grader needs to fend for himself or that your teen with a broken heart should just get over it. Your children need a shoulder to cry on and someone always to listen with love. It's your privilege to provide love as a parent. But it's also your privilege to be a coach and leader who pushes your child to the next level of development.

It's a privilege for the parent both to provide love and to push your child to the next level of development.

Our kids don't need us to be friends first; they need us to be parents first. At the slightest sign of discomfort or hardship, do you swoop in for the save? Obviously you must defend your child against injustice or evil done against them. But when your child forgets a lunch, maybe that's an opportunity for a valuable lesson instead of an extra trip to school for you.

Consider this sign, posted at a boys' high school, which elicited more than 3,900 comments on Facebook: "Stop: If you are dropping off your son's forgotten lunch, books, homework, equipment, etc., please turn around and exit the building. Your son will learn to problem-solve in your absence."[1]

It reminded me of the first time Ethan forgot his water bottle at middle school. My heart sank when I saw the tall, icy bottle on the breakfast table. Ethan rides his bike to school, and it was a hot day in August. Should I go to school with his water bottle? I decided not to. When I asked him after school how he survived the heat without water, his answer was chill. "It was fine, Mom. They have water fountains at school."

Another day, he left his school-issued iPad at home. I paced the floor, looked for his schedule, and wondered if he might have a test that would require his iPad. I contemplated driving to school. My stomach was in knots. He didn't have a phone, but I figured he'd borrow one if he needed his tablet. He arrived home hours later, cool as a cucumber. "Was it okay without your iPad?" I blurted out. "It was fine, Mom," he answered calmly. "Don't worry. I can take care of it."

MOM TO THE RESCUE!

Ladies, we especially like to rescue our children. We are born nurturers. I can't tell you how many times I've said, "It looks a little cold this morning. I can drive the girls to school." James just takes down the bikes from the garage and tells the girls to start pedaling. I sit beside Lucy, trimming her fingernails when I know she can do it herself. I wash the dirty, crusty pots and pans, leaving the easier dishes for the kids. Moms tend to make the road easier, while dads tend to push for the ascent. Like one of the first times Ethan mowed the lawn. I saw him struggling to get the grass out of the bag into our garbage can. I quickly and instinctively moved toward him, holding the garbage can open while pounding on the bag so the grass would fall.

"What are you doing?" James asked me.

What I didn't know was James had just left Ethan alone to solve this dilemma. When James rounded the corner to see *me* doing the job, he was mystified. Moms (and dads too), we must have the self-control to do less so our kids can learn to do more. The struggle is part of growing up. When James sees Ethan besieged with grass, he smiles and thinks, "My son is becoming a man."

Child-development researchers Foster Cline and Jim Fay coined the term "helicopter parent" in 1990 to refer to a parent who hovers over a child in a way that runs counter to the parent's responsibility to raise a child to independence.[2] Hovering is much more than being an involved parent. Consider this study where children and their parents were invited to sit in a lab. Children were encouraged to complete as many puzzles as they could in ten minutes. Parents were permitted to help their kids, but they were not encouraged to do so.

The parents of children with social anxiety touched the puzzles significantly more than other parents. They attempted to help when their kids did not ask for help. You can see how years of this kind of hovering can lead to an anxious child who looks to a parent for help and guidance instead of learning how to play and solve problems on his or her own.[3]

Apparently we don't just fly close to our young kids. Julie Lythcott-Haims served as dean of freshmen and undergraduate advising at Stanford University. In her book *How to Raise an Adult: Break Free of the Overparenting Trap and Prepare Your Kid for Success*, she writes about her experience with college students:

> My colleagues and I at Stanford began to notice a new phenomenon—parents on the college campus, virtually and literally. Each subsequent year would bring an increase in the number of parents who did things like seek opportunities, make decisions, and problem solve for their sons and daughters—things that college-aged students used to be able to do for themselves. This was not only happening at Stanford, mind you; it was happening at four-year colleges and universities all over the country.[4]

Why do we over-involve ourselves as parents? Maybe our parents weren't there for us, and we don't want to make that same mistake, so we overcompensate. Or perhaps we derive our significance from parenting. We don't want to find ourselves out of a job. Or maybe we're worried our children can't succeed in this tough world without us pulling a few strings.

Kendra Smiley warns parents of running to teachers to change grades or manipulating awards. Kendra says, "When that child has success, the kid won't believe he did it on his own. He'll think, 'I'm sure mom or dad went in and that's how I got the award.' They can't even enjoy and appreciate their success. Do you want to rob your child of the pleasure of success, or do you want to rejoice with both of you knowing he did it on his own?"[5]

When you boil it down, you want the best for your son or daughter. I believe we all eventually come to this conclusion: preparing our sons and daughters to be independent adults is more important than pampering and babying them as children.

START WITH CHARACTER

Legendary basketball coach John Wooden said, "Be more concerned with your character than your reputation, because your character is what you really are, while your reputation is merely what others think you are."[6] Kids can easily place more emphasis on appearance and reputation especially because of social media. As a parent, you must continually swing the pendulum back to character. Your child's future success rises and falls on character. Is your child trustworthy? Is your child grateful and good? Does your child work hard? What is your child like when no one is watching?

Years ago, James and I were blessed to hear the famous football coach Lou Holtz share his three rules of life at a conference:

Rule #1: Do the right thing.

Rule #2: Do everything to the best of your ability with the time allotted.

Rule #3: Show people you care.

We adapted these rules and applied them to our household, teaching our kids from a young age to practice these four core values:

R: Do what's Right.

O: Do to Others as you would have done to yourself.

B: Do your Best.

S: Smile.

James created this acronym ROBS to remind us that when we do less than this, we rob God and others. I wrote in my journal about a hard day with Lucy when she was in second grade:

Lucy has been very negative and hard on herself lately. She'll say things like, "I can't do it" and "I'm the slowest." She overreacts when provoked by a sibling. She took more than thirty minutes to finish her smoothie. I gave her an assignment as a result to write an essay completing the sentence, "Instead of getting angry or frustrated, I will . . . " She cried many tears about this task and finally sat down with a piece of paper for about twenty minutes.

Here's what she wrote (unedited):

Instead of getting angry or frustrated, I will be pacient. I will not get angry by using self-talk (talking to yourself). Also I could count down from 10. And I could take a deap breath.

Instead of getting angry, I will think of good thing not negitive things.

I was so proud of her discoveries. She couldn't wait to read the letter to James. Look at her statements within the grid of our four character rules:

Do what's right: It's the right thing to learn to control your negative emotions.

Do to others: She will be less angry at family members.

Do your best: Being patient is giving your best.

Smile: I'll think of good things and not negative things.

At bedtime that night, I told Lucy reading her letter was the highlight of my day. She said, "It's easier to be cheerful when you have God in your heart. When you don't have God in your heart, it's not easy. You can choose to be happy, but it's hard." Isn't that the truth? We have a distinct advantage as Christians: the Holy Spirit can help us do what we can't do in our own strength.

> **The Holy Spirit can help us do what we can't do in our own strength.**

We use our four rules to guide the rewards and consequences the kids receive. If they lie about something, we go to the four rules and ask, "Which rule(s) did you break by lying?" Rewards work this way too. One of my favorites is when James hides cash under random objects that need attention. For example, each Friday we receive a community newspaper in the driveway. James put $5 under the newspaper, waiting to see who would pick up the paper and get the money. Ethan kicked the newspaper, which led to him finding the $5. We gave him the benefit of the doubt that he was actually going to pick up the paper after he kicked it! Cleaning up around the house, even when it's not a job assigned to you, shows you care and that you're doing your best and doing what's right.

TAKE THE ACRONYM CHALLENGE

James and I came up with the ROBS acronym that's worked so well with our children. What basic rules and core values do you want to emphasize in your home? Do a bit of advance brainstorming, and then take one evening to work with your spouse (or even with your kids, if they are older and insightful) to come up with an acronym that fits your family's style and goals.

Our family acronym has only four letters. I'd highly recommend keeping it short so your children can easily memorize and repeat it. Possible starting words: HONOR, GRACE, JOY, GIVE, HELP.

Character is often forged in the heat of adversity. When Ethan was in kindergarten, he broke his right leg and had to wear a cast for six weeks. The doctor assigned a wheelchair to keep Ethan comfortable, but James would have nothing to do with that. He knew Ethan needed exercise to quicken his healing. We left with crutches instead. When the cast came off, Ethan had to do physical therapy that was quite boring, repetitive, tedious, and difficult for a little boy. But we saw in the weeks that followed that the difficulties Ethan had to overcome with his leg had a positive effect in his life.

He had worked his self-discipline muscle for weeks. When it was

Character is often forged in the heat of adversity.

time to sit down for homework, practice the piano, or respond to a disappointment, he was more patient and capable of adjusting. The physical pain and inconvenience of wearing a cast toughened him up in a good way. Dan Kindlon, a child psychologist and lecturer at Harvard, said,

> It's like the way our body's immune system develops. You have to be exposed to pathogens, or your body won't know how to respond to an attack. Kids also need exposure to discomfort, failure, and struggle. I know parents who call up the school to complain if their kid doesn't get to be in the school play or make the cut for the baseball team. I know of one kid who said that he didn't like another kid in the carpool, so instead of having their child learn to tolerate the other kid, they offered to drive him to school themselves. By the time they're teenagers, they have no experience with hardship. Civilization is about adapting to less-than-perfect situations, yet parents often have this instantaneous reaction to unpleasantness, which is "I can fix this."[7]

Parents, let's not fix everything. Instead, embrace failure, struggle, and hardship as very useful teachers in our children's lives. This is not about uncaring parenting; it's about parenting that cultivates character.

SKILLS PAY THE BILLS

As James teaches our kids a new skill such as unloading the dishwasher, he'll exclaim in a funny voice, "Skills pay the bills!" Brainstorm with your spouse some tasks that your

children may be ready to tackle with more independence
to prepare them for life. Here are a few starting ideas:

- Putting away toys
- Packing his or her own lunch
- Doing laundry
- Choosing outfits
- Riding a bike safely in a neighborhood
- Cleaning the bathroom
- Cooking a meal
- Navigating conflict with siblings or friends
- Setting homework goals
- Reviewing movie and TV choices

PARENT WITH A PLAN

The book of Judges ends with these sad words: "In those days there
was no king in Israel; everyone did what was right in his own eyes"
(Judg. 21:25 NKJV). Unlike the former days when Moses and Joshua
led and the people followed God's laws, this was a dark period in
Israel's history when everyone did whatever felt right. There was a
vacuum of godly leadership very much like today.

Parents, we must rise.

Are you a leader who parents with a plan in your home? Zig
Ziglar said, "If you aim at nothing, you will hit it every time."[8] I know
it's much more convenient to go with the flow, taking each day as it
comes. But you don't hit many targets on purpose that way. Many of
us live day-by-day in survival mode, not significance mode. Thank-
fully a few small changes made with the end in mind can make a huge
difference in your child's future.

Do you have a child who can't sit in a restaurant without playing video games or using a phone? You've just discovered your next small step: to retrain your child to sit and talk with people without a digital device. Does your child always "forget" to do his or her chores? It's time for a consequence to remember. Tired of seeing our puppy's water bowl empty, James charged a $10 fee for the empty bowl. That was a hefty fee in their economy, but the bowl gets filled up now.

Keep your eye on the prize: a mature, godly, grateful, hardworking young adult who's able to live independently from Mom or Dad. The child of generations ago could map out adulthood by societal norms: complete high school, leave home, get a job, find a spouse, and have children. In 1960, 77 percent of women and 65 percent of men had achieved all five milestones by age thirty. But in 2000, just half of thirty-year-old women and one-third of males had passed these milestones.[9]

According to a 2015 US census report, about one-third or twenty-four million young adults, ranging in age from eighteen to thirty-four, lived with their parents.[10] Why are so many young adults not launching out on their own and creating their own families?

Some may answer, "Millennials are lazy," "The job market has changed," or, "It's the economy." These reasons may help us to cope, but blaming our circumstances or making excuses won't help our children advance at work and life. We've got to present our children one option: in our home, you must grow up. There is no Plan B of prolonged adolescence.

DO MORE WITH LESS

Parenting is like a funnel, wide at the top and narrow at the bottom. When your children are young in the wide part of the funnel, your involvement is substantial. You're choosing what clothes they wear, what food they eat, when they eat it, and exactly who is allowed to play with them. You are proactive in feeding your child's mind. What books are they reading? What music do they sing? What positive experiences will you share? You're enforcing boundaries and loving with all you've got. As your kids get older and move down the funnel toward adulthood, you do less and less. You leave more decisions to your children. Your fingerprints aren't over everything anymore. They're old enough to leave their own fingerprints now.

Dannah Gresh remembers when her girls were tweens and teens. They would come home and say, "Everyone is watching this movie." Dannah would pull up the movie on a review site like Plugged In, and they would read the review together. She would ask her daughters what they thought. "Put them in the driver's seat of the decision-making when they are ten or eleven. Make sure you stay in the passenger seat for a while as they're still learning how to drive."[11]

I experienced this recently with Noelle. We pulled up reviews for the movie her friends were all talking about. Just based on the movie poster she said, "Oh, I don't want to see that." I want Noelle to know we can always look up what's popular at her school and talk about it together. I started to play the movie trailer. "Really, Mom," she interjected, "I don't want to watch that!" I was happy Noelle could make the decision on her own to skip watching the movie. It showed me if you feed your children good moral entertainment when they're young, they will take that sensibility and those taste buds into their tween years and beyond.

During the years when your children are in middle school and high school, you are wise to transfer more financial responsibility to them (some sixth graders may also be ready for this). Many college students say they wish they had learned more about personal finances before leaving home. You don't want a shiny credit card to be the first experience your college freshman has with managing money. Mary Hunt, author of *Raising Financially Confident Kids*, gave each child a "salary" and made them "money managers." I like these titles, which confer an air of importance. Each child was required to give 10 percent and save or invest 10 percent. The rest was theirs to use for items and events that parents would no longer be paying for. You might determine these items to be school supplies, clothes and shoes, concert tickets, fast food, birthday gifts for friends, etc. We implemented this plan when Ethan started eighth grade.

Our family is frugal. Ethan's feet are growing so quickly, it seems like it's always time to look for new shoes. I found a generic brand of tennis shoes, completely made with white leather for only $17. I put them in my shopping cart, astounded at the deal. We had a good laugh. I fully admit for a middle-school boy, these "old-man"-looking tennis shoes were ugly and pathetic. But since he had been dubbed a money manager and given a salary, he put the shoes in his closet. After all, it was his money, not ours, he was now using to buy shoes.

You can teach your young children to divide money into three containers: one for saving, one for giving, and one for spending. When your credit card bill comes in the mail, talk about how debt and interest work. Show them you tithe at church and give offerings to missions. During the high school years, make it a priority to attend Financial Peace University with your kids (or have them attend alone if you've already done it). This nine-lesson money management course taught by Dave Ramsey is hosted throughout the United States and available anytime online.[12]

As your children get older, they need you to do less for them. Oh, they still need you close by as a mentor and confidante, but they don't need you micromanaging money, homework, laundry, or friendships. Your constant input can be crippling, not caring. Psychologist Michael Anderson shares an illustration from his office, working with families of adolescents for fifteen years. He asks parents,

If we drew up a contract here that if your child had a 3.4 grade point, you would agree to never mention school to them, would you sign the contract? The interesting thing is in all these years, 90 percent of them won't sign the contract because they want the right to badger their kid about homework, whether the kid is doing well or not.[13]

It's a sobering observation. Our constant input can be an issue of control, not caring. We can get used to supervising our children and all that surrounds them, perhaps thinking we will keep them safe. What if we as parents are contributing more than our fair share to the prolonged adolescence of young people today? It's time for us to stand up and leave the room. Let's see what our kids can do on their own. You may be surprised to see how far they can fly.

Parents Rising Question
Would you describe yourself as a helicopter parent, a hands-off parent, or somewhere in-between?

Parents Rising Prayer
Lord, forgive me if I've done too much or too little for my child. I ask You to build strong character in my son or daughter. May my child grow up to be a mature, godly, grateful, hardworking young adult who is able to live independently with great success. In Jesus' name, amen.

Parents Rising Action Step
What is the next thing your child needs to learn in life to prepare for adulthood? It might be doing laundry, packing a lunch, or driving a car. Make plans to teach that skill beginning this week.

Conclusion: Dream Big

Through you we push back our enemies;
through your name we trample our foes.
I put no trust in my bow,
my sword does not bring me victory;
but you give us victory over our enemies,
you put our adversaries to shame.

Psalm 44:5–7

When Ethan turned twelve, we planned a ceremony to celebrate his journey to manhood. No girls were allowed, including me. The men took care of everything from grilling mouthwatering ribeye steaks to organizing laser tag in the park. I was told the best part of the evening happened sitting around a bonfire. Twelve men spoke words of affirmation and wisdom into Ethan's life. These men included James and my dad, church friends, a former neighbor, and Royal Ranger commanders (similar to Boy Scouts).

"You have to have a vision for your life. What do you want to become? Now is the time to make plans," my father said. "When I was your age living in Indonesia, I was dreaming about coming to America and becoming a doctor. Keep in mind, my parents didn't even have the money to travel to the next town."

Another piece of advice from our friend Tim stood out to Ethan: "When you are deciding on a college, visit churches in the area.

Being established in a local church is especially important during the college years." Tim was an excellent student; he was accepted at Harvard and Johns Hopkins. Yet his advice to Ethan was spiritual in nature. Today Tim (or Dr. Mim as baby Ethan used to call him) is a highly respected medical doctor and a strong believer.

Our boys and girls desperately need this kind of positive affirmation and direction for the future. They don't need to grow up being constantly told about "grim prospects," "the poor economy," or "the shrinking job market." They need to be encouraged to honor God, dream big, and increase their skills to match their dreams. As Noelle's favorite speaker, Jim Rohn, said,

> If you talk to your children, you can help them keep their lives together. If you talk to them *skillfully*, you can help them to build future dreams. Dreams get you started; discipline keeps you going (emphasis mine).[1]

Are you encouraging your son or daughter to dream about the future? I hope so. Perhaps you've downplayed dreaming because you know the truth. Kids can't really become anything they want. Your son who is 5'8" isn't going to become an NBA basketball player no matter how much he dreams. We can become *too* realistic. Who's got the time or heart to lasso the moon anymore?

But the Bible does say nothing is impossible with God (Luke 1:37 NKJV). With intellectual honesty you can tell your child, "Keep dreaming of becoming the next great novelist, singer, movie director, or astronaut. Work on your craft and plan a backup job!" Childhood is for dreaming, and we need to encourage big dreams in the hearts of our little children. We should be our kids' loudest cheerleaders and biggest fans. I love the sign radio host and author Jim Burns has in his office. It's yellowed with age and reads, "Every child needs someone who is irrationally positive about them."[2]

THERE'S MORE TO LIFE THAN SAFETY

Mothers, and fathers too, can elevate safety—not dreaming—above everything else: whatever you do, just be safe. I remember riding my bike to school with the girls. As I put my foot in the pedal to return home, one of my mom friends said, "Ride carefully."

Ride carefully.

I chewed on those words all the way home. They bugged me. I knew what she meant and agreed with her sentiment. *Look both ways before crossing a street. Watch out for cars. Be mindful of your downhill speed.* But those words seemed to sum up the loudest advice today's parent gives to a child: Ride carefully. Be safe.

Be safe isn't a very motivating mission statement to build a life around (although it would work well for a skydiving company). No one pays money to see a movie where the main character remains safe from trouble and conflict. We know about many heroes from the Bible, not because they played it safe, but because they displayed courage in the face of fear. Maybe instead of sending our kids off to school with "Be safe," we should say, "Be courageous."

This isn't about fostering recklessness or foolishness. It's about teaching our kids to stretch beyond what's comfortable, and to be brave in order to do what's right. Daniel 11:32 says, "The people who know their God shall be strong, and carry out great exploits" (NKJV). Our children can walk through life with confidence because God is with them. What if young Johnny heard each day "Be strong in God" instead of "Be

> **Our children can walk through life with confidence because God is with them.**

careful"? What kind of difference would it make in his attitude and experience?

BEHOLD AND BEWARE

Jim Rohn said, "The two great words of antiquity are *behold* and *beware*. Behold the possibilities and beware the temptations."[3] When you read these two words in the Bible, pay close attention because something important will follow.

Psalm 127:3 says, "Behold." Lean in. A central idea is about to be introduced by the writer Solomon: "Behold, children are a heritage from the LORD, the fruit of the womb is a reward. Like arrows in the hand of a warrior, so are the children of one's youth" (Ps. 127:3–4 NKJV).

Your children are not a burden; they are a blessing. They aren't meant to bring you stress; they were created to bring you joy. They are useful like arrows. As the Jeremiah Study Bible notes, "An arrow goes to a place the archer cannot go to accomplish a purpose the archer cannot accomplish. With God's help, Christian parents raise their children in such a way that they become arrows sent out to do good for God."[4]

Behold the possibilities in your child's future and the good they can accomplish!

Remember my father and his desire to come to America? As you can guess, his crazy dream did come true. He and his pregnant wife left Indonesia for New York while they were in their twenties. I was born in America. My parents couldn't speak English very well. If you would have told them their baby girl would someday become an author, they might have said, "Why not?" They were dreamers.

Behold, there are grand possibilities in your child's future. Dream on, and pass optimism to your kids.

The other great word of antiq- **There are grand**
uity isn't as pleasant: *Beware*. We like **possibilities in your**
behold, but we can bury and forget **child's future. Dream**
beware. We find it in many verses in **on, and pass optimism**
the Bible such as in Deuteronomy **to your kids.**
6:12: "Beware, lest you forget the
LORD who brought you out of the land of Egypt, from the house
of bondage" (NKJV). This warning followed the Jewish Shema that
parents were to pass along to children, to "love the LORD your God
with all your heart and with all your soul and with all your strength"
(Deut. 6:5). If you don't heed the warnings of the bewares in the
Bible, your family will head down a path of devastation.

We must especially beware when we are doing well, in good
health with bread on the table. That's when we can forget to pray,
stand guard against evil, and fully depend on God. Keep on the look-
out for things that threaten the spiritual health of your child. Beware
of what sin you allow to remain in your personal life because your
children want to grow up to be like you.

Just like what one boy wrote in a compilation book called *Children's Letters to God*: "Dear God, I want to be just like my daddy when
I get big but not with so much hair all over. Sam."

Another boy wrote, "Dear God, How come you did all those
miracles in the old days and don't do any now? Seymour."[5]

Guess what, Seymour? God still does miracles today, healing
broken bodies and broken families. As we near the end of our book
journey together, may your heart be filled with hope for your home.
Plan for big wins as you put these eight strategies into play:

#1 Amusement is not the highest priority.
#2 Parents call the shots.

#3 Routine and boundaries provide security.

#4 The Bible and prayer every day.

#5 Marriage takes a front seat.

#6 Good food served on the table.

#7 Love is spelled T-I-M-E.

#8 Launching adults, not babying children.

Parents, we must rise! There is no better time than now. You've *moved from a lower position to a higher one, increased in fervor and intensity, become heartened,* and have joined many other concerned moms and dads to *increase in number.*

Together we stand with the common mission of raising kids who love God, respect authority, and value what's right.

When Lucy turned seven, she paused for a few moments before blowing out her birthday candles. She looked up and said, "I want to tell you my wish. I wish I would follow Jesus for the rest of my life and shine as a light for Him." This is also my greatest wish, and I believe it is yours too. With every birthday, we get another year to influence our children to love the Lord and shine. Let us not waste our moments.

Parents, it is up to us. It's our time to rise.

Parents Rising
Manifesto

I suggest you read this declaration aloud with confidence every Sunday or Monday morning as you begin a new week of parenting.

I am a thoughtful, decisive, honorable, hardworking parent who is committed to raising children who love God, respect authority, and value what's right. I provide guidance, leadership, and wisdom for my sons and daughters. I clearly understand it's my job to teach my children right from wrong. I take full responsibility for their training. I will lead with love, laughter, grace, forgiveness, boundaries, and consistency. I spend time with my child instead of catching up on my phone or watching TV.

I understand I am raising a future adult. I am not afraid to make unpopular decisions for the eternal good of my child. I will not allow my child to be addicted to phones or tablets. I will limit screen time. I will serve nutritious food and ensure my children get regular exercise. I insist my children demonstrate respect for me and other adults such as teachers, pastors, and coaches. I teach my children to value marriage and desire the blessing of having a family of their own. I pray and read the Word of God to gain direction for my life.

I will not make excuses. I will not wallow in guilt. I will not stop, shut up, back down, or waver in the face of opposition, discouragement, or pushback from my kids. I admit I am fully dependent on God and walk confidently with Him. I will rise to do my best to raise my children to honor God and will leave the results in His hands.

Introduction:
Why You Must Rise

1. Have your children ever stood in defiance and said, "Make me"? Maybe they didn't use those exact words, but the attitude was there. How do you respond when your kids challenge your authority?

2. Do you agree with the statement, "The health of a family rises and falls with leadership"? Why or why not?

3. What would it look like to be a servant leader in your home?

4. What is one win—one fantastic change—you would like to experience in your family as a result of reading this book?

Strategy #1: Amusement Is Not the Highest Priority

1. How much screen time do your children typically get each day? What are they usually doing on a device (texting, homework, social media, video games, watching TV, etc.)?

2. Why do you think it's harmful for a child to be constantly amused? Or why do you think it's okay?

3. If you had a digital Sabbath for one day without Wi-Fi, phones, or any screen time, how would your children do?

4. Can you tell if any of your children are addicted to video games or their phone or tablet?

5. Does your son or daughter have access to a screen in his or her bedroom? Where are your children's devices overnight?

Strategy #2: Parents Call the Shots

1. Who calls the shots in your home on most days: you or your kids?

2. Do you need to be more softhearted or strict with your children?

3. Why is obeying the fifth commandment to "honor your father and your mother" so important in the healthy development of your child? What do they lack if they disobey that command?

4. Do your children regard you as a leader in the home?

5. How will you become a stronger leader to your children?

Strategy #3: Routine and Boundaries Provide Security

1. Would you describe your family schedule as routine or chaotic right now?

2. What time do your kids go to bed? Is the bedtime ritual consistent throughout the week?

3. What are some rules and boundaries that have really worked well?

4. What are some new rules you need to make (or old ones that need to be enforced)?

5. How are you promoting modesty in dress and dating attitudes with your kids?

Strategy #4: The Bible and Prayer Every Day

1. Do your children observe you reading the Bible and praying on a regular basis?

2. Research suggests the most important faith influence on your child's life comes from you as a parent. How should that impact your words and actions?

3. Were you raised by Christian parents who passed down faith to you? If so, how did they do it? If not, what changes do you want to make in raising your children?

4. What evil in the culture makes you angry as a parent? How can you protect your children from things like pornography, drugs, gender confusion, video-game addiction, and cyberbullying?

Strategy #5: Marriage Takes a Front Seat

1. Think back to your dating and newlywed days. How has your romance been affected by having children?

2. Does your spouse feel he or she has to compete with the kids for your attention?

3. How often do you go out on dates? Plan your next date. What would a great date look like?

4. Will your children be excited about getting married based on your example?

Strategy #6: Good Food Served on the Table

1. How are your kids doing on a scale of 1 to 10 with eating nutritious foods?

2. How many meals a week do you eat together as family?

3. Do you need to improve the quality of your conversation around the table? Who usually talks? Who needs to be prodded to share?

4. Are there screens present during mealtime?

5. When was the last time you invited someone over for dinner? Why is hospitality important for kids to experience?

Strategy #7: Love Is Spelled T-I-M-E

1. What are some of your favorite ways to spend time with your children?

2. What could you eliminate from your day to get an extra fifteen minutes to play and talk with your kids?

3. In a study of six thousand children, more than half said their parents checked their phone too often. What would your kids say?

4. Are you a good listener?

5. Are you willing to invest the time necessary to train your children in the next set of skills they need to know?

Strategy #8: Launching Adults, Not Babying Children

1. When you look at your son or daughter, do you see a future adult or only a child?

2. If your child forgot his or her homework, would you drive it to school?

3. When are you tempted to swoop in and rescue your child? How often do you or your spouse act as helicopter parents?

4. Are you afraid of becoming obsolete (outdated, useless) when your kids grow up?

5. What are the character traits that are important to your family? Does your family have core values or a mission statement?

Conclusion: Dream Big for Your Home

1. Are you a dreamer? What are your dreams for your children?

2. Do you think we have elevated safety too much? Are kids as resilient, daring, and courageous as in past generations?

3. Children indeed are a blessing. Share things you are grateful for as a parent.

4. How has reading this book changed your perspective as a parent? What will you do differently as a result?

Acknowledgments

I am able to write because of the amazing support of my family. A big thank-you to my parents, Peter and Ann. They live five minutes away and fill in all the gaps from taking care of the kids to feeding us like royalty. My parents raised me to love God, respect authority, and value what's right, and I'm forever grateful. Another big thanks to James's parents, Arthur and Marilyn, who raised James to become a strong and loving husband and father.

Thanks to the excellent team at Moody Publishers. I am indebted to John Hinkley, Zack Williamson, and Janis Todd for your vision and support. Thank you to my editor, Annette LaPlaca, for being so competent and easy to work with.

Thank you to my friends who generously gave their time to lend their wisdom to this book: Dr. Gary Chapman, Dr. Todd Cartmell, Dannah Gresh, Dr. Kathy Koch, Fern Nichols, Kendra Smiley, and to many who told me their stories.

Thank you to my wise and godly prayer team for lifting up *Parents Rising* and ministry events in prayer. Thank you also to my Moms in Prayer group. Knowing we have agreed in prayer about our kids makes all the difference in the world.

Thank you to James and our three children, Ethan, Noelle, and Lucy. For two weeks straight, you took care of dinner and pushed me out of the kitchen so I could finish writing. James, your old-school parenting ideas are working marvelously. Yes, you are a genius, and

I'm madly in love with you. Ethan, you kept me on target with your question, "How many words did you write today?" Noelle and Lucy, you know how to rock a book table. Thank you so much for letting me share your childhood stories from the past with our reader friends. I love you all!

Notes

Introduction

1. *The American Heritage Dictionary of the English Language*, s.v. "rise," https://ahdictionary.com/word/search.html?q=rise; *Merriam-Webster*, s.v. "rise," last updated February 15, 2018, https://www.merriam-webster.com/dictionary/rise.
2. Chip Ingram, *Culture Shock: A Biblical Response to Today's Most Divisive Issues* (Grand Rapids: Baker, 2014), 38.
3. Ibid., 19.
4. "CDCs Abortion Surveillance System FAQs," *Centers for Disease Control and Prevention*, January 6, 2017, https://www.cdc.gov/reproductivehealth/data_stats/abortion.htm.
5. "Unmarried Childbearing," *Centers for Disease Control and Prevention*, March 31, 2017, https://www.cdc.gov/nchs/fastats/unmarried-childbearing.htm.
6. *Merriam-Webster*, s.v. "rise," last updated February 15, 2018, https://www.merriam-webster.com/dictionary/rise.
7. Ibid.
8. Zig Ziglar, *BrainyQuote*, https://www.brainyquote.com/quotes/quotes/z/zigziglar378592.html.
9. *Merriam-Webster*, s.v. "rise," last updated February 15, 2018, https://www.merriam-webster.com/dictionary/rise.
10. Ibid.

Strategy #1: Amusement Is Not the Highest Priority

1. Gary Chapman and Arlene Pellicane, *Growing Up Social* (Chicago: Moody, 2014), 129.
2. Kaiser Family Foundation, "Generation M2: Media in the Lives of 8- to 18-Year-Olds," *KFF.org*, January 20, 2010, http://kff.org/other/event/generation-m2-media-in-the-lives-of/.
3. Dr. Archibald Hart and Dr. Sylvia Hart Frejd, *The Digital Invasion: How Technology Is Shaping You and Your Relationships* (Grand Rapids: Baker, 2013), 63.
4. Iowa State University, "Nearly 1 In 10 Youth Gamers Addicted To Video Games," *ScienceDaily*. www.sciencedaily.com/releases/2009/04/090420103547.htm.
5. Adam Alter, *Irresistible: The Rise of Addictive Technology and the Business of Keeping Us Hooked* (New York: Penguin Press, 2017), 229.
6. Nick Bilton, "Steve Jobs Was a Low-Tech Parent," *New York Times*, September 10, 2014, https://www.nytimes.com/2014/09/11/fashion/steve-jobs-apple-was-a-low-tech-parent.html?_r=0.
7. Neil Postman, *Goodreads.com*, https://www.goodreads.com/author/quotes/41963.Neil_Postman.
8. Olawale Daniel, "The Average Number of Screens in a Home Has Increased," *TechAtLast*, June 27, 2014, http://techatlast.com/average-number-of-screens-in-home-increased/.

9. Dr. Kathy Koch, personal interview, April 26, 2017.
10. Erma Bombeck, *ThinkExist*, http://thinkexist.com/quotation/in_general_my_children_refuse_to_eat_anything/205241.html.
11. Anne Fishel, "The most important thing you can do with your kids? Eat dinner with them," January 12, 2015, *Washington Post*, https://www.washingtonpost.com/posteverything/wp/2015/01/12/the-most-important-thing-you-can-do-with-your-kids-eat-dinner-with-them/?utm_term=.8981f970650d.
12. P. Matthijs Bal and Martin Veltkamp, "How Does Fiction Reading Influence Empathy? An Experimental Investigation of the Role of Emotional Transportation," *Plos*, January 30, 2013, http://journals.plos.org/plosone/article?id=10.1371/journal.pone.0055341.
13. E. A. Vandewater, D. S. Bickham, J. H. Lee, H. M. Cummings, E. A. Wartella, and V. J. Rideout, "When the television is always on: heavy television exposure and young children's development," *American Behavioral Scientist*, 2005, 48 (5): 562–77.
14. "Reading to Young Children," *Child Trends Databank*, June 2015, http://www.childtrends.org/?indicators=reading-to-young-children.
15. Laura Clark, "Gadgets blamed for 70 per cent leap in child speech problems in just six years," *Daily Mail*, December 27, 2012, http://www.dailymail.co.uk/news/article-2253991/Gadgets-blamed-70-cent-leap-child-speech-problems-just-years.html.
16. "Reading to Young Children," *Child Trends Databank*, June 2015, http://www.childtrends.org/?indicators=reading-to-young-children.
17. Lecia Bushak, "E-Books Are Damaging Your Health: Why We Should All Start Reading Paper Books Again," *Medical Daily*, January 11, 2015, http://www.medicaldaily.com/e-books-are-damaging-your-health-why-we-should-all-start-reading-paper-books-again-317212.
18. Brandon Keim, "Why the Smart Reading Device of the Future May Be . . . Paper," *WIRED*, May 1, 2014, http://www.wired.com/2014/05/reading-on-screen-versus-paper/.
19. Ibid.
20. Erik Kain, "'Grand Theft Auto V' Crosses $1B in Sales, Biggest Entertainment Launch in History," *Forbes*, September 20, 2013, https://www.forbes.com/sites/erikkain/2013/09/20/grand-theft-auto-v-crosses-1b-in-sales-biggest-entertainment-launch-in-history/#2fc96e1e2b22.
21. Malathi Nayak, "FACTBOX—A look at the $66 billion video games industry," *Reuters*, June 10, 2013, http://in.reuters.com/article/gameshow-e3-idINDEE9590DW20130610.
22. Adam Alter, *Irresistible*, 17.
23. Jane McGonigal, "Gaming can make a better world," *TED*, 2010, https://www.ted.com/talks/jane_mcgonigal_gaming_can_make_a_better_world/transcript.
24. Mike Flacy, "Netflix rolls out 'post-play' to keep you watching endlessly," *Digital Trends*, August 15, 2012, https://www.digitaltrends.com/home-theater/netflix-rolls-out-post-play-to-keep-you-watching-episode-after-episode/.
25. Bianca Bosker, "The Binge Breaker," *The Atlantic*, November 2016, https://www.theatlantic.com/magazine/archive/2016/11/the-binge-breaker/501122/.
26. Neil Postman, *Goodreads*, https://www.goodreads.com/work/quotes/2337731-amusing-ourselves-to-death-public-discourse-in-the-age-of-show-business.

Strategy #2: Parents Call the Shots

1. Lori Gottlieb, "How to Land Your Kid in Therapy," *The Atlantic*, July/August 2011, https://www.theatlantic.com/magazine/archive/2011/07/how-to-land-your-kid-in-therapy/308555/.
2. Stephanie Wood, "The Secret to Self-Esteem," *Parenting*, 2017, http://www.parenting.com/article/the-secret-to-self-esteem.
3. William Chisteson, Amy Dawson Taggart, and Sore Messner-Zidell, "Too Fat to Fight: Retired Military Leaders Want Junk Food Out of America's Schools," *Mission: Readiness, Military Leaders for Kids*, 2010, http://cdn.missionreadiness.org/MR_Too_Fat_to_Fight-1.pdf.
4. Dr. Leonard Sax, *The Collapse of Parenting: How We Hurt Our Kids When We Treat Them Like Grown-Ups* (New York: Basic Books, 2016), 7.
5. John Rosemond, personal interview, January 30, 2015.
6. Sax, *The Collapse of Parenting*, 160.
7. Dr. John Townsend, *Boundaries with Teens* (Grand Rapids: Zondervan, 2006), 200.
8. John Rosemond, personal interview, January 30, 2015.
9. *The Lion King*, directed by Roger Allers and Rob Minkoff (1994; Walt Disney Pictures/Buena Vista Pictures), DVD.
10. Sax, *The Collapse of Parenting*, 7.
11. Dr. Gary Chapman, personal interview, August 14, 2013.
12. Townsend, *Boundaries with Teens*, 34.
13. Winston Churchill, *BrainyQuote*, http://www.brainyquote.com/quotes/authors/w/winston_churchill.html.

Strategy #3: Routine and Boundaries Provide Security

1. Archibald D. Hart, "Bedtime Rituals," *Focus on the Family*, 2010, http://www.focusonthefamily.com/parenting/parenting-challenges/time-for-bed/bedtime-rituals.
2. Dr. Gary Chapman, personal interview, August 14, 2013.
3. Dr. Todd Cartmell, personal interview, March 21, 2017.
4. Ibid.
5. Ibid.
6. Dennis Rainey, *Aggressive Girls, Clueless Boys* (Little Rock, AR: Family Life Publishing), 2012.
7. Dannah Gresh, personal interview, April 4, 2017.
8. Ibid.
9. Ibid.
10. Josh McDowell, *Goodreads*, https://www.goodreads.com/quotes/264719-rules-without-relationship-leads-to-rebellion.

Strategy #4: The Bible and Prayer Every Day

1. Dr. Kara Powell and Dr. Chap Clark, *Sticky Faith: Everyday Ideas to Build Lasting Faith in Your Kids* (Grand Rapids: Zondervan, 2011), 15.
2. Ibid., 24.
3. Bob Smietana, "Study: Americans fond of Bible, but how many read it?" *Baptist Press*, April 25, 2017, http://www.bpnews.net/48743/study-americans-fond-of-bible-but-how-many-read-it.
4. Dr. Kathy Koch, personal interview, April 26, 2017.

5. Dr. Gary Chapman, personal interview, August 14, 2013.
6. *Merriam-Webster,* s.v. "rise," last updated February 15, 2018, https://www .merriam-webster.com/dictionary/rise.
7. Dave Thier, "'Grand Theft Auto 5' Has Sol Nearly $2 Billion at Retail," *Forbes,* May 13, 2014, https://www.forbes.com/sites/davidthier/2014/05/13/grand-theft-auto-5-has-sold-nearly-2-billion-at-retail/#5911eb413d30.
8. Beverly LaHaye Institute, "Facts about Pornography," *Concerned Women for America,* May 2011, http://concernedwomen.org/wp-content/uploads/2013/11/ CWA_FactsAboutPornography.pdf.
9. Kendra Smiley, personal interview, April 5, 2017.
10. Arlene Pellicane, *31 Days to Becoming a Happy Mom* (Eugene, OR: Harvest House, 2015), 98.
11. Dr. Kathy Koch, personal interview, April 26, 2017.
12. Fern Nichols, personal interview, April 4, 2017.
13. Ibid.

Strategy #5: Marriage Takes a Front Seat

1. Dannah Gresh, "Getting Lost in God's Love" (part 2 of 2), *Focus on the Family* broadcast, April 30, 2013, http://www.focusonthefamily.com/media/daily-broadcast/getting-lost-in-gods-love-pt2.
2. Linda Dillow and Lorraine Pintus, *Intimate Issues: 21 Questions Christian Women Ask About Sex* (Colorado Springs: Waterbrook Press, 1999), 68–69.
3. Dr. David Clarke, personal interview, March 28, 2011.
4. Charles R. Swindoll, *Strike the Original Match* (Grand Rapids: Zondervan, 1993), 31.
5. Dr. Emerson Eggerichs, *Love and Respect: The Love She Most Desires; The Respect He Desperately Needs* (Nashville: Thomas Nelson, 2004), 16.
6. Laura Petherbridge, personal interview, August 6, 2014.
7. Janet Thompson, personal interview, August 25, 2014.
8. Ashleigh Slater, *Team Us* (Chicago: Moody, 2014).
9. Kendra Smiley, personal interview, April 5, 2017.
10. Gretchen Livingston and Andrea Caumont, "5 facts on love and marriage in America," *Pew Research Center,* February 13, 2017, http://www.pewresearch.org/fact-tank/2017/02/13/5-facts-about-love-and-marriage/.
11. Nancy Jo Sales, "Tinder and the Dawn of the 'Dating Apocalypse,'" *Vanity Fair,* September 2015, https://www.vanityfair.com/culture/2015/08/tinder-hook-up-culture-end-of-dating.
12. Dr. Gary Chapman, personal interview, August 14, 2013.

Strategy #6: Good Food Served on the Table

1. Dena Kleiman, "In a Time of Too Little Time, Dinner Is the Time for Family," *New York Times,* December 5, 1990, http://www.nytimes.com/1990/12/05/ garden/in-a-time-of-too-little-time-dinner-is-the-time-for-family. html?pagewanted=all.
2. Lydia Saad, "Most U.S. Families Still Routinely Dine Together at Home," *Gallup News,* December 26, 2013, http://www.gallup.com/poll/166628/families-routinely-dine-together-home.aspx.
3. Sharon Jayson, "Each family dinner adds up to benefits for adolescents," *USA Today,* March 24, 2013, https://www.usatoday.com/story/news/nation/ 2013/03/24/family-dinner-adolescent-benefits/2010731/.

4. "Why is family dinner so important?" *The Six O'Clock Scramble*, http://www.the scramble.com/family-dinner-challenge-statistics/, accessed September 5, 2017.
5. Lisa Lewis, personal interview, April 10, 2017.
6. Ibid.
7. Lisa Lewis, *Healthy Happy Cooking* (Galveston, TX: First Place 4 Health, 2016), 200.
8. Mary L. Gavin, M.D., "Overweight and Obesity," *KidsHealth from Nemours*, October 2016, http://kidshealth.org/en/parents/overweight-obesity.html.
9. "Report Says 75 Percent of Young Americans Unfit for Military Service," *Fox News Politics*, November 5, 2009, http://www.foxnews.com/politics/2009/11/05/new-report-says-percent-young-americans-unfit-military-service.html.
10. Kim Painter, "The whole world has a weight problem, new report says," *USA Today*, May 28, 2014, https://www.usatoday.com/story/news/nation/2014/05/28/world-obesity-report/9675267/.
11. Dr. Gary Chapman and Ramon Presson, *101 Conversation Starters for Families* (Chicago: Northfield, 2012), 2.
12. Asheritah Ciuciu, *Full: Food, Jesus, and the Battle for Satisfaction* (Chicago: Moody, 2017), 211.
13. Mother Teresa, *Goodreads*, https://www.goodreads.com/quotes/139677-the-greatest-disease-in-the-west-today-is-not-tb.

Strategy #7: Love Is Spelled T-I-M-E

1. Zig Ziglar, *Goodreads*, https://www.goodreads.com/author/show/50316.Zig_Ziglar.
2. Dr. Kathy Koch, personal interview, April 26, 2017.
3. Kendra Smiley, personal interview, April 5, 2017.
4. Dr. Todd Cartmell, personal interview, March 21, 2017.
5. Ibid.
6. Ibid.
7. Eryn Lynum, *936 Pennies: Discovering the Joy of Intentional Parenting* (Bloomington, MN: Bethany House, 2018).
8. Health Enews Staff, "Kids Resent Parents Who Are Glued to Their Phones, Study Finds," September 29, 2015, http://www.ahchealthenews.com/2015/09/29/kids-resent-parents-who-are-glued-to-their-phones/.
9. Dr. Kathy Koch, personal interview, April 26, 2017.
10. http://quotes.land/no-symphony-orchestra/.
11. Dr. Todd Cartmell, personal interview, March 21, 2017.
12. Ibid.
13. Dannah Gresh, personal interview, April 4, 2017.
14. Warren Buffet, *BrainyQuotes*, https://www.brainyquote.com/quotes/quotes/w/warrenbuff409214.html.
15. Earl Nightengale, *BrainyQuotes*, https://www.brainyquote.com/search_results.html?q=time.

Strategy #8: Launching Adults, Not Babying Children

1. Moriah Balingit, "'Your son will learn to problem-solve.' Arkansas school puts helicopter parent on notice," *Washington Post*, August 19, 2016, https://www.washingtonpost.com/news/education/wp/2016/08/19/your-son-will-learn-to-problem-solve-arkansas-school-puts-helicopter-parents-on-notice/?utm_term=.81c30718b63e.

2. Julie Lythcott-Haims, "The four cultural shifts that led to the rise of the helicopter parent," *Business Insider*, July 9, 2015, http://www.businessinsider.com/the-rise-of-the-helicopter-parent-2015-7.

3. Joel L. Young, M.D., "The Effects of 'Helicopter Parenting,'" *Psychology Today*, January 25, 2017, https://www.psychologytoday.com/blog/when-your-adult-child-breaks-your-heart/201701/the-effects-helicopter-parenting.

4. Julie Lythcott-Haims, *How to Raise an Adult: Break Free of the Overparenting Trap and Prepare Your Kid for Success* (New York: St. Martin's Griffin, 2015), 4.

5. Kendra Smiley, personal interview, April 5, 2017.

6. John Wooden, *Goodreads,* https://www.goodreads.com/author/quotes/23041.John_Wooden.

7. https://www.theatlantic.com/magazine/archive/2011/07/how-to-land-your-kid-in-therapy/308555/. June 5, 2017.

8. https://www.goodreads.com/quotes/78121-if-you-aim-at-nothing-you-will-hit-it-every, June 6, 2017.

9. Lythcott-Haims, *How to Raise an Adult,* 77.

10. Jonathan Vespa, "The Changing Economics and Demographics of Young Adulthood: 1975–2016," *The United States Census Bureau, report #P20–579*, April 2017, https://www.census.gov/library/publications/2017/demo/p20-579.html.

11. Dannah Gresh, personal interview, April 4, 2017.

12. Financial Peace University, Dave Ramsey, https://www.daveramsey.com/fpu.

13. "Rethinking Your Parenting Strategies," (part 1 of 2), *Focus on the Family broadcast,* May 10, 2016, http://www.focusonthefamily.com/media/daily-broadcast/rethinking-your-parenting-strategies-pt1.

Conclusion

1. Jim Rohn, *AZ Quotes,* http://www.azquotes.com/author/12558-Jim_Rohn/tag/dream.

2. Jim Burns, "Creating Spiritual Rites of Passage for Your Children," *Focus on the Family* broadcast, March 6, 2017, http://www.focusonthefamily.com/media/focus-on-the-family-daily-international/creating-spiritual-rites-of-passage-for-your-children.

3. Jim Rohn, *AZ Quotes,* http://www.azquotes.com/quote/1334679.

4. Dr. David Jeremiah, *Jeremiah Study Bible NKJV* (Franklin, TN: Worthy Publishing, 2013), 794.

5. Stuart Hample and Eric Marshall, *Children's Letters to God* (New York: Workman Publishing, 1991).

About the Author

Arlene Pellicane is a speaker and author of several books including *Calm, Cool, and Connected: 5 Digital Habits for a More Balanced Life*; *31 Days to Becoming a Happy Mom*; *31 Days to a Happy Husband*; and *Growing Up Social: Raising Relational Kids in a Screen-Driven World* (with Dr. Gary Chapman). She has been featured on the *Today Show*, *Fox and Friends*, *Focus on the Family*, and *FamilyLife Today*.

Before becoming a stay-at-home mom, Arlene worked as the associate producer for *Turning Point Television* with Dr. David Jeremiah. Arlene earned her BA from Biola University and her masters in journalism from Regent University. Arlene lives in San Diego with her husband, James, and their three children. Find out more at ArlenePellicane.com.

FOR THOSE FEELING OVERLOADED WITH TECHNOLOGY...

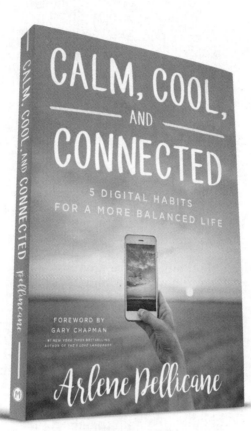